WALKING WITH THOSE WHO WEEP
A Guide To Grief Support

Walking With Those

WHO WEEP

A Guide To Grief Support

by

Don & Ron Williams

RonDon Books

62 Ridgecrest Lane
Killen, Alabama 35645

WALKING WITH THOSE WHO WEEP
A Guide To Grief Support

10th printing, 2017

A Product Of

Sain Publications

P.O. Box 616 – Pulaski, TN 38478

(931) 363-6905

Dedicated To

Joe and Dot Williams

Their lives have been spent in loving their children–
Loving their God–
Loving Christ's Church–

They have served as models for their children
in showing what it means to care for others.

We are eternally grateful to love them as our parents.

Don and Ron Williams

Table Of Contents

Acknowledgments

This book is the result of a lot of hard work and effort. It could have never come together if not for many people *"behind the scenes"* working to make it possible. At the risk of leaving out someone, we would like to acknowledge some very special people.

First and foremost, besides our God, we would like to thank our wives and children for being patient with us as we wrote this book. Leisa, Matt and Ben, and Bonnie, Jon Michael and Stephen have been very supportive in allowing us the time away from them in teaching grief classes, being involved in chaplain programs, listening to the heartaches of others, etc. Were it not for their love, devotion, and understanding, this book would not have been written. Leisa and Bonnie, as school teachers, were very helpful in proofreading and making suggestions concerning the content. Bonnie's knowledge as a English teacher proved especially invaluable with grammar, writing usage, and editorial comments. Her expertise in this field was of inestimable worth.

We thank *Bill McDonald* for providing the inspiration for us to be involved in grief work. His friendship through the years has been greatly appreciated, and his expertise in the field of grief counseling has aided us greatly in our own development in this ministry.

We thank *Kim Black* for her wonderful artistic abilities in drawing and designing the front cover. She took an idea and made it much better than anyone else could have done. She is a terrific artist!

Special thanks goes to *Paul Sain* for going the "extra mile" in helping us complete this project in an efficient and timely way. His expertise and advice was greatly valued!

We thank the elders and members of the congregations where we have served as ministers for having the vision to see that grief work is a part of the ministry of a preacher. Because of the foresight of the elders of the Guin Church of Christ, North Carolina Church of Christ (Don), and the Evergreen Church of Christ (Ron), we have been able to work and broaden our abilities to help in the lives of hurting people.

Last, but not least, we are forever grateful *to the many people who have opened their hearts and lives* and allowed us to experience some of the pain they feel because of the losses they have sustained. A great number of people have been a part of the grief community classes that we have taught over the last five years, and they have taught us volumes about caring, grief, and about how to survive, even when one's world is seemingly falling apart. We will always be indebted to these wonderful, loving people, and it is because of them that this book is written.   Don & Ron Williams
October, 1996

Chapter 1

What Happens When Your World Crashes In?

The Enormous Pain Of Grief

by Ron Williams

"Grief is like being in a deep dark pit with no way out," the couple from a grief support class wrote. In asking my class participants to write down in their own words the meaning of grief, the couple added,

> Grief is a feeling of being under a dark veil that you cannot lift. There is a feeling that there is something heavy across your heart and a tight band that is around your head. Grief is total despair. Grief is a feeling of helplessness that seems unbearable.

The above-mentioned definition is a heart-felt meaning of what happens when grief invades a person's or family's life. Grief, from the Latin word, *gravis*, means "heavy." Indeed, if there has ever been an understatement for a word, that has to be one! Grief is one of the most debilitating expressions of emotion that a person can ever imagine. Grief is an all-encompassing emotion that can cause a person to feel as if all of the problems of the world have suddenly been placed upon their back and on their heart!

Webster's New Collegiate Dictionary defines grief as a "deep and poignant distress caused by or as if by bereavement."[1] In my work with people that have dealt with the loss of something or someone precious to them, I have found grief to be an individual experience, generally a painful feeling of sadness that usually follows an actual loss or precedes an anticipated loss.

Please notice the emphasis that I have given to the idea of grief being a loss of SOME THING as well as SOME ONE! So often we think of grief as being "one-dimensional," while grief is experienced in so many other areas of a person's life besides the death of an individual. While it is true that we normally think of grief when a loved one dies, grief is just as prevalent over the loss of other things as well.

For example, imagine you returned home from your vocation today and discovered your house being totally consumed by fire. Wouldn't there be some sort of real grief involved in your dealing with that loss? Definitely so! Maybe you built that house with your own hands-maybe you sub-contracted the building of that house and you and your mate labored many long hours on working on that project. Although your loss did not involve your death or any of your family members, your loss is GREAT because something that was significant to you has been destroyed!

1996 will be remembered by many people in our country as the Year of the Downsizing of American Companies. How do you think those employees felt when they arrived at work one day to be given the news that they no longer had a job? In the part of the state where I reside, a number of factory employees received notice in the winter of 1995 that their jobs would be terminated in a few months. Imagine what those employees were faced with in thinking about holiday buying! Don't you think that those individuals, their mates, and children felt real pain and grief over the reality of being "let go" from a job they depended on for their livelihood! Of course they would!

What would happen to you tomorrow if some medical

problem began to totally debilitate you? Wouldn't you feel anger, resentment, depression, and grief over the good health you USED to have and the bad health you are now experiencing? Obviously, you would! Often when I visit people in hospitals, I will find them feeling distressed over their medical problems that have invaded their lives. Such feelings are a normal reaction to the loss of a healthy lifestyle that enabled that person to do what they wanted to do in life.

One of the greatest losses that a person could ever experience in life is the tremendous pain that can come from• divorce. Consider the person that marries an individual that they truly love and want to grow old with this mate. Imagine one day that something happens that begins to cause friction and ill will toward that marriage partner. Gradually, or perhaps, suddenly, the couple (or at least one of them) begins to pull away from their marriage commitment. Soon what used to be "married bliss" become a "declaration of war" as each person attacks and fights against the other. Maybe counseling is tried but one or the other refuses to work on the problems within their life. Soon lawyers are called, moving plans are made for one of them, and soon, a piece of paper arrives declaring that the marriage is legally over!

Although each person may be glad that the ordeal is finally over, soon the feelings of grief and despair may begin to set in. These emotions of grief may seem overwhelming as the person begins to deal with the reality of their divorce. People I have worked with have compared their divorce to that of an actual death of a person. The problem though, is that when a person that we love dies, we typically bury them out of our sight. In divorce, although the relationship has died, the person (previously their mate) is not dead but very much alive and still may be a constant irritation in their life! Thus, many powerful feelings of grief may be experienced as the person deals with the death of a marriage and the end of the most intimate of all relationships.

Individuals that lose a part of their body due to some disease like cancer or someone that loses some part of their body due to an injury can often experience a great expression of grief. We often take our bodies and our health for granted. When a person loses some part of their body, they may feel "very depressed" and feel as if a death has occurred to them, for in reality, that is exactly what has happened!

Expectant parents that experience the trauma of the miscarriage of their child often feel the frustration of a real loss in their lives. Unfortunately, many well-meaning people make the matter worse by the things that they say to these grieving parents. Such statements as "You can always have other children," or "Well, you didn't want this child if it wasn't right," do nothing but add to the hurt and grief that these parents are feeling. These parents are dealing with the exhausting pain of loss because they feel cheated–cheated from enjoying the most unique reward of being a parent-that of bringing a child into the world!

A pet can be a great companion to people of all ages. Imagine you have a pet that lives with you and your family in your house. Imagine your children play constantly with that pet, they bathe it, and it sleeps in the children's room with them. Now imagine what would happen if that pet suddenly got sick and died. You know exactly what would happen in your house, don't you? Your house would become flooded with a river of tears due to the loss that your family has experienced!

Humans are not the only ones that grieve when we lose some animal that we have loved. I know of a lady that had a cat and dog that she had raised together for many years. These pets were constant companions to her and to one another as well. They ate together out of the same bowl, slept in the same place, and traveled with the lady where ever she went. The dog eventually grew sick and was near death. The veterinarian did everything he knew to save the animal but to no avail. A few days after the dog died, the woman noticed that her cat was acting peculiar. She refused to eat, to play, or to do anything that it had previously done. Being worried about the animal, the lady took the pet to the veterinarian and asked for the doctor to do everything possible for her. After tests and a thorough examination, the doctor told the woman that there was nothing physically wrong with the cat except that it was grieving itself to death due to the loss of her fellow companion, the dog. Sure enough, in just a few days, the cat wandered off and disappeared, and was never seen again. The doctor guessed that the cat had gone off somewhere alone to die. As you might suspect, the woman grieved over the loss of both animals for a long period of time.

Hopefully you have seen wherein we have tried to show that grief is felt by many kinds of losses other than the death of a person. Although the death of a person is certainly traumatic, these losses that have been discussed are just as painful when they occur in a person's life. Other losses such as the pain that many people may feel when they move from a familiar place to an unfamiliar one, or the loss that retirees sometime feel when they leave their vocation of life after many years, are traumatic feelings as well.

When any of these losses occur in our lives, we need someone that will love us and care for us. We need someone that will try and understand why we are grieving over some devastating loss in our lives. We offer these ideas from the THEOS International Foundation as something to think about in helping others with some loss in their life.

"JUST WALK WITH ME"

I have a problem. I want to tell you about it. No, I really don't. I'd rather keep it to myself; handle it alone. I do think it would be good for me to share it with you, though. I don't want to because I'm afraid of what you'll say or how you'll act.

I'm afraid you might feel sorry for me in a way that makes me feel pathetic–like I'm some 'poor thing.'

I'm afraid you'll try to cheer me up. That you will give me words, or texts or prayers that tell me in a subtle way to stop feeling bad. If you do that I'll feel worse (but hide it behind my obedient cheerful smile). I'll feel you don't understand. I'll feel you are making light of my problem (as if it can be brushed away with some brief words of cheer).

I'm afraid you'll give me an answer. That this problem that I've been wrestling with for some time now and about which I have thought endless thoughts will be belittled. You can answer in a half-minute what I've struggled with for weeks?

I'm afraid also you might ignore my problem; talk quickly about other things, tell me of your own.

I'm afraid too you might see me stronger than I am. Not needing you to listen and care. (It's true, I can get along alone, but I shouldn't have too.)

What I'd really like is if you would "just walk with me." Listen as I begin in some blundering, clumsy way to break through my fearfulness of being exposed as weak. Hold my hand and pull me gently as I falter and begin to draw back. Say a word, make a motion, or a sound that says, 'I'm with you." If you've been where I am tell me how you felt in a way that I can know you're trying to walk with me—not change me.

But I'm afraid...

You'll think I'm too weak to deserve respect and responsibility...

You'll explain what's happening to me with labels and interpretation...Or you'll ask me, 'What'ya going to do about it?'

PLEASE, just walk with me. All those other things seem so much brighter and sharper, and expert. But what really takes love is to 'Just Walk with Me.'

I'm sure, what I want is people who have a Shepherd as their model. People who in their own way bring to others an experience of: 'The Lord is my Shepherd, I shall not want...Yes, even when I walk through the valley, You're with me (walking with me).[2]

WORKS CITED

1 **Webster's New Collegiate Dictionary**. (1975). Springfield, MA: G. & C. Merriam Company, p. 505.

2 **THEOS International Foundation**. "Just Walk With Me," Suite 105, 322 Boulevard of the Allies, Pittsburg, PA 15222-1919, 414-471-7779.

AUTHOR'S NOTE: Throughout this book the **New King James Version** and **King James Version** are used in Scripture references.

Chapter 2

What Is This "Monster" Called Grief?

The Total Possession And Reality Of Grief

by Don Williams

Jeff was the first person, as well as the first man, to become a part of the first class I taught on grief (names have been changed to respect their identity). He was married to a wonderful lady, and they had a beautiful daughter with whom to share their lives.

In his words, "My life came crashing in when we learned that my wife had terminal cancer. We prayed, and I was told that if I believed hard enough, she could be made well. We prayed, but it was not enough." His wife died within a year, leaving him behind with an adolescent daughter. Later, as he was describing his world, he defined grief in this manner: "Grief is like waiting for an important phone call that never comes!"

Another dear, sweet christian lady lost her husband in a homicide murder. Near Christmas, as her husband was putting together a tricycle for a grandchild, three men broke into the house, cutting off all the power. When the husband went to see what was going on, they jumped him in the yard, cutting him with a machete-like instrument. When she tried to run for help, they surrounded her vehicle and forced her back inside. Then they took all her jewelry, as well as the money bag from their business.

About a year and a half after her husband's death,

she wrote me, thanking me for the class and telling me of her "new life." The trial was now over, she had sold their home and the business, and she had relocated. As she told me of her different life, she put it this way, "I still sometimes have trouble getting zoomed in."

What did Jeff and this good christian lady mean? How could death and grief be so devastating? Doug Manning, in his book **Don't Take My Grief Away from Me**, describes the feeling when he writes:

> Right now your chest hurts—the numbness has worn off and real pain has replaced it. You wonder if you will ever be well again. A thousand questions flood your mind. A thousand hurts pop up every day—Every day you find a new thing to cause memories and bring tears. You find it hard to sleep. The awful loneliness seems to be there every moment of every day. The finality of death leaves a hollow feeling all over your body. Loneliness comes in one size- Extra Large.[1]

The two above true stories could be compounded over and over. I have had the occasion of talking with and learning from courageous parents who have had to endure the terrible loss of children, whether it be from cancer or terrible accidents. I have sat and listened to older and younger women and men talk about life without their beloved mate by their side and in their life. I have listened as devoted adult children talked of life without a loving mother and father in their lives any longer. No more would there be a parent to call for advice, a "cheerleader" for the kids or grandkids. The pain of their loss was difficult, almost impossible to bear.

Some have had the sad experience of having multiple losses occurring one after the other. One good christian friend lost her mother, sister, husband, and best friend—

all in less than one year! Another lady I knew lost both parents, a close uncle and aunt, and a invalid brother— all in about three years. Betty Jane Spencer lost four sons who were shot and killed in an execution-style massacre in rural Indiana. She was wounded but survived. In looking back on her losses, she put it this way: "I was killed too. I just didn't die."[2]

It is this all-encompassing feeling that one must go through as they enter into the valley of grief. Illnesses of any type are bad; cancer and heart trouble have the ability of wearing folks down. Yet, people with cancer can go into remission, and individuals with heart trouble can be made better. With death, there is no remission, or return to good health. In John 11, Lazarus got a second chance at life as Jesus called him forth out of his four-day-old tomb. Today, sadly, there is no such recourse. Therese Rando, in commenting on the total possessive nature of grief, writes,

> It is a whole host of emotions ranging from anxiety to anger to guilt to confusion to relief and more...it reaches into every part of your life, touching your work, your relationship with others, and your image of yourself...you can expect grief to have an effect on you psychologically, socially, and physically.[3]

HOW GRIEF AFFECTS YOU PSYCHOLOGICALLY

Grief is a cruel teacher, sending its students into a myriad of emotions. Unlike an illness, these emotions stay with you constantly, usually for a long period of time. People in my grief class have likened their mannerisms to that of a robot. They feel as if they are going through the motions, as if what they are doing is like a nightmarish dream, a dream they hope is not real.

Their emotions cause them to be laughing one moment, crying hysterically the next, and then thinking "it is really not true" the next moment. These emotions, later discussed in chapter four, cause grievers to literally think that they are "losing their minds."

HOW GRIEF AFFECTS YOU SOCIALLY

Grief affects one socially, in that it changes the entire nature of one's life. When someone loses a loved one to death, especially if the death was sudden and unexpected, it is as if someone has turned their world upside down. One cannot think and reason as before. It is not possible to be the person they were before that death. In many cases, one gives up the desire to live. As Sissy Thomas put it,

> When I was given the news of my son's death, I felt as if I, too, had died. As the hours dragged into days, then months, I felt myself wanting to do nothing but give up and die myself. I could focus on nothing but what my son had to face that morning and all that he had lost...I resigned myself to stay and do my time until it was my turn to die...[4]

This embodiment of grief gives a person little energy to deal with the everyday decisions of life. Often, one desires to escape from life and those who would live it. "They" may have come to the funeral and helped in many other ways, but they "HAVE GONE BACK" to their normal way of living. A person in grief lacks all motivation and direction to deal with other people or other matters.[5]

HOW GRIEF AFFECTS YOU PHYSICALLY

It is not atypical to hear those involved in the "journey of grief to say," I have never been as physically and mentally exhausted as I have in the valley of grief."

As human beings, our minds and bodies are linked together. In some cases, physical manifestations of grief are the only way in which one allows their grief to be expressed. One might ask them how they are doing, and they will commonly express the sentiment, "Fine." From all outward expressions, they may appear to be fine. They may even look and seem as if they are "their old selves" again. But away from the office at work, or away from their "worn placid smile" at church, they are inwardly and physically hurting. Anorexia, ulcers, decreased energy, apathy, sleep difficulties (too much or too little, interrupted sleep)-all of these are common physical ailments and concerns that come with grief.

Other physical abnormalities that can occur are weight loss or weight gain, the tendency to sigh, heart palpitations, trembling, shaking, hot flashes, smothering sensations, dizziness, chest pain, pressure or discomfort. These and many other ailments can be the lot of one who is regularly confronted with this "monster" called grief.

Studies have been conducted that show that those in grief have lowered resistance and increased vulnerability to all types of illnesses. One often hears of older couples who lived together for fifty years or longer. Suddenly, one of them dies, and the other one cannot make it without them. They "grieve themselves" to the point of becoming ill, and in a short period of time, die themselves.[6]

SUDDEN VERSUS ANTICIPATED DEATH, AND WHAT IT DOES TO GRIEVERS

Someone has well said that "grief comes in one size-extra-large." I have heard people discuss that some deaths are worse than others. I try to tell people that the worst loss is their loss, whatever that is. Death is tragic, life-altering, and final.

Some will argue that one manner of death is worse than another. That is, some suggest that unexpected death is worse than a death that is expected. Proponents of this school of thought will say, "at least you got to say good-bye. You had the opportunity of being there when they died. We did not have that chance. They died without any loving family member present."

Others who lost a loved one through a terminal illness may feel differently about which is worst. They may believe that a sudden death is less painful than the one they have had to endure, perhaps thinking of an illness that has lasted for years (one can begin to grieve even when the loved one is still alive, but dying). They might argue,

> ...at least you did not have to see your loved one suffer and waste away. You did not have to deal with the painful recognition that they were dying, and that there was little you could do. You did not have to wait for it to happen.[7]

THE ARGUMENT IS A MOOT POINT! THE DEATHS OF THOSE WE LOVE, NO MATTER HOW IT HAPPENED, LEAVES US LONELY AND HURTING! It is important to realize that there are differences between sudden and anticipated deaths. That needs to be understood and recognized.

Let me illustrate sudden, unanticipated loss in this way. Let's say that I am walking down a major street. I am whistling, or my mind is on something else, when all of the sudden, out of the corner of my eye, I see a man running towards me at an angle. I see him coming and realizing he is about to run into me, I brace myself. More than likely, he will knock me down, but at least I know who hit me and what happened.

Now suppose that the same thing happens, but this

time I do not know what happens. I do not see him coming or even hear him coming. The outcome, in both scenarios are the same—I AM ON THE GROUND. But now, with the latter situation I have some additional questions to deal with-what happened, why am I on the ground, why am I bleeding and in pain, etc?

> As a result, the ability to cope with the situation-that is, to decide what to do in response to the blow, is compromised since the shock and unpredictability of it has stunned you so much.[8]

SUDDEN DEATH

As one deals with a sudden, unanticipated death, the ability to cope with the death is diminished because of the nature of the loss. Grievers are shocked and stunned by the sudden loss of their beloved. Recovery is complicated, because one is overwhelmed, not only by the death, but by the how and why of the loss.

In sudden loss, there may be extreme feelings of shock, bewilderment, and anxiety. One has to try to face the massive gap between the way things are (my loved one has died) and the way things ought to be (they should be alive). After a sudden death, the loss does not make sense. Grieving survivors may find themselves telling the story of how their loved one died over and over again. This does two things: it validates the reality of the loss, as well as enabling them to help make some sense of the loss. One may find himself becoming a sort of detective, looking back and trying to see if there were any clues left behind by the deceased. Did they do or say anything that might suggest they were sick or were thinking about their own mortality?

Because there is less factual information to go on,

grievers in sudden losses will take longer to work through grief phases and stages. Shock and numbness often persists longer, because one is not equipped to deal with the sudden death of loved ones. Whereas survivors can successfully work through their grief, dealing with questions about the nature of their beloved's loss, they need to be aware that it "will take longer and demand more from them and from those who seek to comfort them..."[9]

ANTICIPATED DEATH

Although one may have knowledge that their loved one is going to die, such knowledge does not make the loss any easier. Therefore, one can be of great help to himself by being involved in the life of the terminally ill throughout the final journey to death. "It has been well documented by research that your experience in your loved one's dying process will have a profound effect on your grief after his death."[10] Being near them, attending to their needs, making them as comfortable as possible, –all of this helps the survivor as they grieve after the loss of their loved one. It is also beneficial to the dying patient to know that he is loved and cared for to the very end.

In anticipatory grief, there are three kinds of losses. There is past loss where terminal illness causes the loss of the healthy individual that you have loved and known for many years. Cancer and other illnesses can leave only the shell of what was once a vibrant, robust, and energetic person. Grief very often begins while one remains alive, as in the case of a Alzheimer's patient.

There are present or on-going losses. As one continues getting worse, the survivor has to witness the dying person's progressive debilitation, their increasing dependence, and their decreasing control. It is important to any terminal patient that they have as much independence and dignity, for as long as it is possible.

A third type of loss is future loss. Not only is impending death on the horizon, but other losses come as well. Because of one's worsened condition, the family vacation may not ever be taken again. One's condition may cause him to become immobile, thus becoming bedridden. Additionally, social contact with others becomes difficult and may be lost for good. Changes in life-style, the handing over of decision making from one to another; all of these can cause a great deal of pain and inward frustration.[11]

SUMMARY

There are some who have the mistaken idea that death is something that you "get over" in time. They may quote such maxims as "time heals all wounds" or "God does not give anyone that which he cannot handle." Although they may mean well, they are definitely, entirely WRONG. Time may lessen the hurt, but only if one does his/her "grief work,"[12] and spends time in dealing with his/her emotions, as well as the reality of his/her loss.

To "get over" a loved one's death suggests the idea that they were not important or significant to us, as if it was a bad marriage, or a nightmarish experience. As Dennis Klass comments, in regards to the loss of his child,

> ...we can't get over it, because to get over it would mean we were not changed by the experience. It would mean we did not grow by the experience. It would mean that the child's death made no difference in our life.[13]

There are some ancient lessons to be learned from the Talmud, an ancient Jewish writing. When the Jews lost a relative, they would tear their clothing to demonstrate the ripping apart that death brings. Later, they could mend the garment, but the rent had to show outwardly, so that others would realize the fact that life would not be the same after the loss. It was also decided that the garment could never be sold to another person. This would illustrate the fact that the rending and mending that grief brings to one's life cannot be transferred to others. No one can grieve for another.[14]

WORKS CITED

1   Doug Manning, **Don't take my Grief Away from Me**, (Hereford, Texas: In-sight Books, 1979), p. 41.

2   Janice Harris Lord, **No Time for Goodbyes** (Ventura, California:Pathfinder Publishing,1987), p. 2.

3   Therese A. Rando, **How To go on Living When Someone You Loves Dies**, (New York: Bantam Books, 1988), p. 25.

4   Used with Permission by Sissy Thomas, "From the Heart", in **The Compassionate Friends Newsletter**, Orlando, Florida, seen in **The Compassionate Friends Newsletter**, Tuscaloosa, Alabama, May-June 1995, p. 2.

5   Rando, 44,45.

6   Ibid., 45,46.

7   Ibid, 89.

8   Ibid, 90.

9   Ibid, 90-94.

10   Ibid, 94.

11   Ibid, 95,96.

12   Ibid, 16.

13   Used with Permission by Dennis Klass, "Reflections About Time and Change," **The Compassionate Friends Newsletter**, St. Louis, Missouri, seen in **The Compassionate Friends Newsletter**, Tuscaloosa, Alabama, September-October, 1994, p. 4.

14   Ibid, 5.

Chapter 3

Why Didn't I Know This About Death And Dying?

The Facts Of Grief That Every Person Should Know

by Ron Williams

People begin to realize just how uninformed they are when they begin to deal with the reality of grief in their lives. They can read the best books, they can talk with those who have experienced a loss in their lives and still realize how ignorant they are on this important subject. The reason this is the case is because grief cannot be totally learned until it is experienced!

In 1992, I began my first community grief support class that was to last for eight weeks. I had researched my material thoroughly and felt fairly comfortable in dealing with the twenty-five adults that attended these sessions. During this same time, my mother-in-law was dealing with the final stages of lung cancer. After my fourth week of meeting with my class participants, my wife and I received word that her mother had died unexpectedly during a routine minor surgical procedure. After the funeral and spending several days with my wife's family, I returned home and prepared for my next session of my grief support class.

Words cannot express the tremendous difference I felt and the emotions that I experienced as I taught the remainder of these classes! The first four weeks of the class I had taught what I knew about grief from books and other materials. I had taught the class from an intellectual point of view. The last four weeks of the class were altogether different! Grief had taken on a totally different perspective as I was now dealing with grief from an experiencial manner! Only then did I begin to understand how these people in my class were feeling. I realized then just how much I really had not understood about grief until that moment when I felt the reality of grief of losing someone that I loved! Grief took on a totally different perspective at that time, and I completed these classes by discussing grief as it relates to the heart of a person instead of their head! Needless to say, the second half of these sessions were far more effective than the first half had been. Why? Because I had begun to understand what these people who had attended my class were feeling—I felt the trauma and emotions of that monster called grief!

The problem with grief is that it is a cruel teacher of tragedies that occur in our lives. Grief has a way of totally debilitating us by its control over every part and aspect of our lives. Thus, the more one can know about grief and the way that grief affects us, the more knowledgeable we will be in dealing with it as it invades our lives. The following facts I have found to be useful in dealing with grief.

Fact Number One:
Grief is a natural and healthy consequence
that should occur when a loss
has happened in a person's life!

We live in a world where many people do not want to admit their feelings. We like to hide our emotions from others because we are afraid that people will think that we are weak and frail. Many people make the mistake of thinking that if they grieve for a loss in their lives, then they are behaving in an abnormal and unnatural way. Thus, they make the mistake of forgetting that grief is a natural way of dealing with the loss of something or someone that we love. Less we forget, the shortest verse in all of the Bible is perhaps one of the most powerful verses as well, John 11: 35, "Jesus wept." Jesus was not afraid of allowing the Jews and others around Him to see His expression of grief over the death of a dear friend. He cried because He felt the agony that comes from losing a dear friend!

Some people like to pretend and "act better than they feel" when some loss occurs in their life. Instead of grieving and working through their sorrow, they try to act as if everything is back to normal and that they are in control again. Everyone of us should realize that the grief experience is a natural and a very normal response. Grieving is normal, it is healthy, and it should occur when we have been dealt a devastating loss in our lives. Doug Manning in his book **Don't Take My Grief Away**, writes that:

> ...grieving is as natural as crying when you are hurt, sleeping when you are tired, eating when you are hungry, or sneezing when your nose itches. It is nature's way of healing a broken heart.[1]

Fact number one: grieving is a natural and normal way of dealing with any kind of loss!

Fact Number Two:
*Grief affects a person with their whole being:
Emotionally, physically, mentally,
and spiritually!*

Grief has an overwhelming power to inhibit a person in many ways. While there may be some other kind of trauma that is more devastating than grief, I am personally not aware of such. The emotional impact of grief can cause a person to weep uncontrollably one minute and then be totally depressed the next instant. Grief can cause a person to be hyperactive for days at a time followed by days of listlessness and exhaustion with other mood swings mixed in between. A person in grief can be in control of his thoughts at one moment and suddenly some word or some action triggers a response resulting in numbness of mind and body. Thoughts that range from supposed insanity of mind to one's complete control of his mental faculties can fluctuate from day to day as the person deals with his/her feelings of grief. Spiritually, a person can find himself blaming God for all that has happened to them at one moment when in the next few minutes they may be praying to God to help them in their time of need. Regardless of what manifestation of grief you are experiencing, you need to realize that it will affect your entire person. Fact number two, grief will affect a person with their whole being!

Fact Number Three:
Grief is always an individual matter;
You NEVER know how
another person feels!

Grief is as individualistic as the snowflakes that fall from the sky. No person's grief is going to be like some other person's grief. That statement is true even if you and your entire family are grieving over the death of the same loved one. Grief is individualistic because we are all different in our mourning. We all carry into the grieving process a list of values and attitudes that motivate us to deal with the loss in that particular manner.

The old cliche, "I know exactly how you feel," should NEVER be heard by any person that is dealing with grief. It is impossible for one person to know and to understand how another person feels about their grief situation. Just as each person has fingerprints that are uniquely their own, so each person has his own individual way of dealing with grief.

When someone utters those irreverent words to a grieving person, saying, "I know exactly how you feel," they are implying that all grief is generally the same and is easily understood. Such is not the case! There is literally no way that one's grief is the same as another's or that one can know exactly how the other person is feeling. Words are inadequate to describe the emotions that a person has in regard to their feelings of sadness and pain.

Harriet Sarnoff Schiff in her book, **The Bereaved Parent**, begins with a tale of a prince that was running for his life from revolutionaries that were out to kill him. He runs into town and knocks on the door of a peasant man and asks to hide within his house. The man agrees and hides the prince under his bed. Soon after, the pursuers knock down his door and begin to look for their supposed victim. Instead of moving the bed, they jab knives through the mattress, and without finding the prince, soon leave for another house. The prince, pale and shaken, comes out from under the bed and announces to this peasant that he has just saved the prince of the kingdom! The prince, realizing what this lowly peasant had done, announces that he will give him three wishes.

The peasant man first asks for some repairs to be made to his cottage. The prince agrees with this but chastises the peasant for asking for so little a gift. He next asks for the prince to decree that his neighbor that sells the same wares be ordered to move to the other end of town so that the peasant can sell more of his wares. The prince becomes angry at such a petty request and warns him not to use the last wish so foolishly. The peasant man, being a curious sort of fellow, says that he would like to know how the prince felt when his enemies were thrusting their knives through the mattress.

The prince, now outraged that the man would ask such a personal question, orders that his loyal soldiers come and seize this peasant man for his insolence and orders that he will die on the morrow. The next morning, after spending a pitiful night in prison, the peasant man is taken to the scaffold where an executioner is ready to end his life with his sword. When the executioner is about to make the fatal blow to his neck, a soldier rides up and orders the man to stop the execution in the name of the prince. He hands the peasant man a note from the prince that says: "As your final request you wanted to know how I felt under that bed when the revolutionaries came. I have granted your request because now you know!"[2] Obviously the prince knew that there were some feelings of pain and horror that words alone could never describe. The same is true of a person's individual feelings of grief. Fact number three, grief is always an individual matter—no two people ever grieve the same!

Fact Number Four:
A person's grief experience will be directly affected by the significance of that loss!

People will experience emotions of grief based upon the kind of relationship that they have had with the person who died. For example, imagine that you are notified that your cousin that lives out-of-state has died suddenly of a heart attack. Obviously, you are saddened because someone that you were related to has died. However, you don't have many sorrowful pains of grief from this loss because you had only met this cousin two times in your entire life. The intensity and duration of that loss is minimal, because you did not know that person very well at all.

Let's imagine that on the same day that your out-of-state cousin died, that your uncle was killed in a car accident in the same town where your family lives. This uncle was a special relative as he had been a stabilizing influence in your life when your father had died when you were an adolescent. Although you might eventually send a sympathy note to the family of the deceased cousin, your expression of sorrow and grief would be immense for the uncle that had meant so much to you in your life. It would be very safe to say that the duration and intensity of this loss would be far greater than the death of the cousin that you never really knew. Fact number four, a person's feelings of grief will be based upon the significance of the loss they experience!

There are no words that I know of that can prepare a person totally to be ready for the loss of loved one. A person may know intellectually that their loved one that has a terminal illness will eventually or suddenly die. A person may try to get prepared for the ultimate death of that person. They may plan the funeral service, consult a mortician about necessary arrangements, and even inform the family of what will happen in the future. Even though these necessary things need to be done, when that loved one does die, the mourners will be surprised at how lost and empty they feel.

This is not because of any default of character or because they failed to prepare for the death; it is because they have EXPERIENCED the mobster called grief! When grief occurs, everything else that a person does to prepare for the death is eliminated; grief takes over and becomes the overriding factor in the person's life, mind, soul and heart.

When that occurs, remember the four things that have been suggested in this chapter. Remember that the grief experience is a normal and healthy reaction to your lost. Remember that grief will typically encompass your whole being for a period of time. Remember that YOUR grief will be different from any other person around you as you deal with the loss. Don't let others tell you how your grief "ought" to be. Finally, the grief experience will be based on the significance of that loss to your life. As you loved and related to that person in life, so you will grieve to the same extent by their death.

WORKS CITED

1   Manning, Doug. **Don't Take My Grief Away**. San Francisco: Harper & Row, Publishers, 1984, p. 60.

2   Sarnoff-Schiff, Harriet. **The Bereaved Parent**. Penguin Books, 1977, pp. 9-11 of introduction.

Chapter 4

Am I Losing My Mind?
The "Normality"
Of The Phases Of Grief

by Don Williams

We live in a world marked by assumptions. We wake up in the morning and assume that life will be like it was yesterday. We go to bed and wake up, expecting we will wake up, and the sun will rise. We go through our normal routine of getting the kids off to school, going to work, having a normal day, and then returning home for a routine evening of family time together. We assume our continued good health, daily interactions with loved ones, co-workers and friends, and the business-as-usual routine in our job and community.[1]

But then, something happens. It may be an illness that was unexpected and undetected. This is what happened in my family. On a Thursday afternoon, at 12:35 on May 5,1994, my wife called me from the doctor's office with the sudden news; our twelve year old son had developed diabetes and would be a insulin-dependent diabetic the rest of his life. Not only that, his blood sugar was four to five times over the healthy average, and we had to immediately rush him to a major hospital for treatment to prevent him from going into a diabetic coma. We quickly drove to Florence, Alabama, where we would be moving in several months.

My son attends a special camp for diabetics every year. He is making the necessary adjustments of living with his illness. He takes three shots of insulin every day. Recently, he asked his mother, "When you learned

I had diabetes, were you shocked?" My wife tried not to let on just how scared and panicky we really were. We both cried and felt helpless as we tried to learn about a disease that is common among many Americans. In no way am I trying to say that my son's illness begins to compare with the trauma and the heartache of one who has lost a loved one. It does not, but the point is that numbness and shock can come in varying degrees over situations other than death. It did to us on that day.

For others, it may be some sudden tragedy or catastrophic event that transforms their "neatly-packaged life." The news often comes in the form of a late phone call in the night or in the early morning hours. Those who you thought were safe and secure are not, and that is when your world of "assumptions" caves in. It is as if your world has been violated; the neat package of the ways things have been, and the ways things ought to be, is no more. Someone or something has taken you and your world and turned it upside down.

In the movie **Sleepless in Seattle**, Tom Hanks, the main character, is trying to explain to his son about his mother's death. In essence he says, "Mommy got sick—there was nothing we could do. We don't know why, and if we ask why, we will go crazy!"

One may never know *why* a loss occurs, but the fact is that one will ask why. As Doug Manning writes, "You have the right to ask why—you will ask it whether you are given the right or not."[2] Before the time of your loss, there may have never been a thought about how and why people die, but now you think about it, especially if the loss is sudden and unexpected.

A lawyer friend of mine lived less than two miles from his father and mother. One hot summer day a few years ago, his children and parents had been grocery shopping. The father was carrying the groceries up the steps and had reached the front porch. The wife was already inside and the grandkids were outside with the grandfather. A massive heart attack struck the father, and he fell to the porch. Although cardio-pulmonary resuscitation was begun immediately, he was pronounced dead. His death was a great shock to everyone. I had spent some time with this man only a few days before.

About a year later, my friend wrote me, sending me a poem he had written about his feelings of his father's death. The question WHY is seen throughout these poignant words:

> One day I lost a special friend, not so long ago, and why it had to happen, I still don't really know. Our conversation wasn't finished, we had much more to say. It seems that his departing could have come at a later day.

> It is those moments with my friend which I am left to mourn, you see he's always been around, since the minute I was born. Perhaps my friend was needed at some other distant place, but I rely upon his wisdom, and I'd like to see his face.

> Was he really called away, or did he leave by choice? Did I expend his knowledge, or use up all his voice? Did I take his time for granted, or depend on him too much? Did he feel no longer useful, that I didn't need a crutch?

> Perhaps someday we'll meet again so I can understand, why it didn't end exactly the way I'd always planned. Then he can tell me where he went, and maybe even why, He didn't pause for long enough to bid his son good-bye.
>
> Jerry Hester [3]

"Why?" is one of the first questions that will be asked, and will continue to be asked. There will be various phases that a griever will go through, and must go through, in order for there to be appropriate healing. Although some might say that one should keep a stiff upper lip, and get on with their life, "grief is as natural as crying when you are hurt, sleeping when you are tired, eating when you are hungry, or sneezing when your nose itches. It is nature's way of healing a broken heart."[4]

This all-encompassing grief will come in phases, not neat and orderly stages. In times past, grief has been described as stages or states of mind that people go through. Some have assumed from this that these stages are orderly and unvarying. It is thought that all people grieve in the same way on a static, unalterable course, progressing in only one direction with no individual variation.[5] Nothing could be further from the truth. One might progress from one phase to another, or even be in two phases at once. As has been stated in past grief classes that have been taught, "The only script in grief is no script." With this idea in mind, we will examine various phases one might experience. Although these emotions may not be felt by all, most people will experience some of these feelings. This chapter will deal with the immediate emotions in which one finds himself shortly after the death. The next chapter will deal with subsequent emotions that one feels as he/she begin to actively work through his/her grief.

NUMBNESS AND SHOCK

When death takes place, especially if it is sudden and unexpected, one feels shock and numbness. As Earl Grollman writes,

> Nothing seems real. You are not there. People talk to you; you do not respond. You feel as though you are just a spectator. There is a

deadening of feeling. You have lost your ability
to concentrate...you are literally stunned.[6]

Grieving people have stated that even when the death
was expected, or the accident was so serious that no hope
was given by the doctors, still shock set in when they
learned their departed was dead. The word *death* horrifies
us. In society, we dislike the word, so we will camouflage
it by saying that people have "expired," "passed away,"
"passed on," or "departed this life." Eventually, reality
brings us to the point of realizing and saying that our
loved one has died.[7]

John Claypool, a Baptist preacher, wrote a book
entitled, **Tracks of a Fellow Struggler**. In it he records
his thoughts and reactions to the leukemia cancer and
eventual death of his nine and a half year old daughter
named Laura Lue. His thoughts were preached in four
separate sermons, over a period of several years. A month
after his daughter died, he told of the unique numbness
and shock he felt over the impending death that came.

> At the feeling level, I had abounding hope. I
> did not realize how hopeful I really was until
> that Saturday afternoon as I knelt by her bed
> and saw her stop breathing. ...I was the most
> shocked man in the world at that moment. You
> see, deep down, I did not believe she was going
> to die. In spite of all my mind told me, I found
> myself clinging to the hope that any day a cure
> would be found, or that God would see fit to
> heal her miraculously.[8]

You see, when faced with a crisis, a battle takes
place between the heart and the head. The heart deals
with one's feelings and emotions. The head deals with
one's intellect, facts and logical information. When faced
with death, one can logically and intellectually understand
it, but one's heart and its emotions do not want to accept

the inevitable, so at least for a short while the heart wins out. Then shock sets in.

Shock is not always a bad thing. A person with a physical injury may go into shock so that he cannot feel the fullness of pain. A person who is exposed to the outside elements may have his body go into shock for a short period of time. Our bodies and especially our minds go on auto-pilot. The time frame for shock may be anywhere from two hours to two days to two weeks or more. Janice Lord suggests that one's numbness and lack of emotion give others a false sense of one's stability. Some may think you are strong. and that you are doing well, when in fact "you feel like a mechanical robot. When the shock wears off, and you desperately need your friends, they have resumed life as usual, believing that you are doing fine."[9]

Claypool likens the story of Job to the loss of his daughter and says that Job's first reaction was numbness and shock. Job's friends came to sit with him and did so in silence for Job's losses had been so great that, at first, Job could barely take them in.

> There is so much within us that does not want to accept the actuality of it that our unconscious works against our doing so...it is not at all uncommon for a person under the initial impact of loss to be in something of a daze or walking around as if in a dream.[10]

Some have suggested that they would desire to continue in shock and numbness. But sadly, these feelings pass in time, and another emotion begins to take over.

DENIAL

Referred to as the avoidance phase by Rando, this is the period of time when the acknowledgment of the bad news occurs. Your world has just been shaken; although you have heard the news, and even though you have verbally stated that you understand that they have died, still it is not mentally accepted.

During this period one may respond in several ways. A person may be confused and dazed, unable to understand what has happened. If the death were sudden, your responses may be more intense in that you have had no time to prepare for the loss. You may find yourself asking over and over the same information because you cannot yet comprehend the terrible news-your loved one has died![11]

A person may respond by still believing that the news is wrong. Various people have stated that when the news came that their loved one died, they first believed that it could not be true. Bill McDonald, a funeral home director friend of mine, told me of having to tell a wife that her husband had been killed. He went to remove the body from the scene of the wreck, and later spoke to the wife. She said, "Bill, it isn't true, is it? Tell me it is not true—have you seen him?" 'Yes, I have seen him, and I am sorry, but it is true.'" Bill told me that she did not see her husband until twenty four hours later. When she came in and saw his body for the first time, she broke down weeping, and cried out, "It really is him, isn't it?" All that time she was emotionally denying what had actually happened—her husband was dead!

Another response of denial is to speak of the deceased in the present tense. The phone rings and one thinks it will be their beloved calling in. "You have not given up hope that the one you love will return. You live in the past, hoping to bring it back. To think of the present is an act of unfaithfulness."[12]

Some people may be in denial, even when they appear to accept the death and begin to make responsible plans. They appear stoic as they begin to comfort others and make necessary decisions for the funeral. In most of these cases, the loss is recognized but the emotions of grief are consciously put aside as the grievers try to be strong and hold up for themselves as well as for others. This is especially true of men. Because of social conditioning, men think that a show of emotion is taboo and displays weakness. Therefore, the man may placidly go through the motions, making major decisions about the funeral, making preparations for the family, attending to countless details, as if all is well. Well meaning people may say, "You are holding up so well." This does nothing but affirm the way the man thinks he needs to act, and so he will continue to respond as society thinks he should. Such thinking, if continued for a long while, can bring damaging results to the griever.[13]

Denial may reveal itself in other ways, even after the news of the death is intellectually acknowledged. Some, in manifesting denial, may leave the room of their beloved the way it has always been, for months and even years to come. Others may not desire to see family members that resemble the person that died. A mother's thirty-five year old daughter died. The daughter's two girls looked just like the mother. In an effort to deny the loss, the grandmother would not invite the grandchildren to visit her.

At some point, denial will diminish, and the terrible reality of the death will begin to sink in. It is this writer's opinion that some people go through the funeral home experience and even the funeral in a partial state of denial and shock. The time of two to three days from the actual death to the actual burial is often not enough time for one to assimilate what is actually happening: they are burying the one they loved! In some cultures, the funeral is delayed for several days. This may aid in allowing the reality of the loss to gain entrance into their emotions and their lives.

DEPRESSION, LONELINESS, WITHDRAWAL

"What is-what cannot be changed-must be accepted...The funeral is over. The flowers have withered. Now the loss becomes real. Your loved one is dead."[14] Nicholas Wolterstorff, in writing of his son's mountain climbing fall that led to his death, put it succinctly when he wrote:

> I buried myself that warm June day. It was me those gardeners lowered on squeaking straps into that hot dry hole, curious neighborhood children looking down at me, everyone stilled, wind rustling the oaks. It was me over whom we slid that heavy slab, more than I can lift. It was me on whom we shoveled dirt. It was me we left behind, after reading psalms.[15]

Depression, loneliness, and withdrawal causes a great deal of exhaustion to the griever. No longer is there a reason to try and hold up for others. One may crash, and one may crash very hard. The pain is intense, and one may feel that they do not want to see anyone or do anything. It is common to want to do nothing but sleep, without being disturbed or bothered by family or friends.

It is in this phase of grief that the survivors may need the help of others more than ever before. If there are children still at home, then various domestic chores will have to resume such as washing clothes, cooking food, ironing clothes, keeping appointments, etc. It is then when other people can be of great help in aiding the grieving family by doing these necessary things. Food may be of more help at this time than even before the funeral. A person's presence may mean more now that it did at the time of the funeral. Yet, Bill McDonald has stated that 97% of friends stop visiting the family two weeks after the funeral! At a time when friends are needed the most, many have gone back to their normal routine of living.

It is in this time of depression and withdrawal that one feels sorry for himself. Irreversible loss has been sustained, and it was their loss. "My loved one has died. It hurts ME deeply. Part of MY life has changed. I don't know what to do...I-ME-MY. These are the pronouns of grief. Do not feel ashamed at constantly referring to yourself."[16] Grollman continues by saying,

> This depression is not weakness. It is a psychological necessity. It is one of the slow winding avenues of sorrow and loss. It is part of the mournful work of saying 'Good-bye' to your beloved.[17]

It is in this phase that survivors may dream or have nightmares concerning the deceased. They may wake up in the middle of the night thinking that the deceased called out their name. Others may believe that for one brief instant they saw the deceased in a passing car, or at the store. Sadly, the reality of the situation returns, and it is with this return that emotions become so low.

> It is the neverness that is so painful. Never again to be here with us-never to sit with us at the table, never to travel with us, never to laugh with us, never to cry with us...all the rest of our lives we must live without him. Only our death can stop the pain of his death."[18]

As one begins to face the reality of their loss, there seems to be nothing ahead but doom and gloom. There seems to be no light at the end of the tunnel. One thinks life will never be worth living again. It is common to think of one's own death, and to believe that it would be better if it came sooner rather than later. It is common to believe that you will never laugh, never be happy again, and that you will not be able to make it without your beloved with you.

Notice that the word used is the word "common." More than anything, grieving people need to know that their depressing nature and dismal outlook on life is common and normal for those who travel through the journey of grief. Others have felt in similar ways to what they have felt. It is also helpful for them to realize that others have crawled through and out of the pit of grief. It is this hope that can stimulate one to go on, when they might not really want to go on. This hope will be discussed in the next chapter.

WORKS CITED

1 Delores Kuenning, **Helping People Through Grief** (Minneapolis: Bethany House, 1987), p.15.

2 Doug Manning, **Don't Take my Grief Away from me** (Hereford, Texas:In-Sight Books, 1979), p. 48.

3 Poem used with Permission by Jerry Hester about his father, Gerald Hester, May, 1994.

4 Manning, 60.

5 Therese A. Rando, **How to go on Living when Someone You Love Dies**, (New York: Bantam Books, 1988), p. 20.

6 Earl A. Grollman, **Living when a Loved One has Died**, (Boston: Beacon Press, 1977), p. 22.

7 Earl A. Grollman, Editor, **What Helped Me when my Loved One Died**, (Boston:Beacon Press, 1981), pp. 5,6.

8 John Claypool, **Tracks of a Fellow Struggler**, (Waco, Texas: Word Publishing, 1974), pp. 70,71.

9 Janice Harris Lord, **No Time for Goodbyes**, (Ventura, California: Pathfinder Publishing, 1987), p. 19.

10 Claypool, pp. 95,95.

11 Rando, 20,21.

12 Grollman, Living,   25,26.

13   Rando, 21.

14   Grollman, Living, 48,49.

15   Nicholas Wolterstorff, **Lament for a Son**, (Grand Rapids:Wm. B. Eerdmans, 1987), p. 42.

16   Grollman, Living, 12.

17   Ibid, 45.

18   Wolterstorff, 15.

Chapter 5

Will I Ever Laugh Again?
The Phases Of Grief
On The "Other Side"

by Don Williams

The last chapter ended with the grieving survivor feeling like he is doing anything but surviving. He may want to do anything but live. Life has become so unfair to him, and he does not know why. He wants to know why, but does not have the capacity to begin the search for the answer. In time, whether it be in days or in weeks, he will begin that search for "the truth" as to what happened.

I recall a Christian lady in one of my grief classes that began that "search" three weeks after her husband's funeral. The doctor told the wife that her husband was getting better, and that in a matter of days he would go home from the hospital. Instead, he got worse and died. When she tried to talk to the doctor, the nurse said that she would have to make an appointment with him. She made the appointment, met with the doctor and questioned him as to what happened. The doctor chastised her, telling her she needed to get on with her life and not "travel down some pity road." Her response to him was, "I am not traveling down some pity road–I am just trying to find out what happened to my husband!"

In time, one will leave the phase of withdrawal, and actively begin the journey that ultimately leads them to recovery and reconciliation. It is not a short journey, and in many ways, it is never completed. It is a journey that must be taken if healing and happiness is going to come one's way. The following are some of the phases that one will encounter along the way.

PANIC, ANXIETY, AND ANGER

As reality becomes more and more constant, emotions of withdrawal are replaced by emotions of anger and a endless panic. Someone you loved has died, and you want to know why. You want someone to come up with answers as to why this atrocity could have ever taken place. Questions about the death, especially if it was sudden and unexpected, will consume your thoughts. You want to know how, why, when, what, etc., and you want to know right now!

You will question anyone who will listen to you. That may include the police, doctors, paramedics, the funeral home, the preacher, and, yes, even God. Although it is natural to want to find out all that you can concerning one's death, it has been this writer's assessment that grieving families do not find out much of the information that they desire about the death. Some questions about death cannot be answered. In some cases, the wherefores and the whys and the hows cannot be known. This tends to add to the emotional stress that grief brings with the death experience.

Your anger and questioning may be directed at the deceased. You want to know what they were thinking. Nicholas Wolterstorff, in writing on the death of his mountain-climbing son, suggested these questions:

> Why did he do it? Why did he climb the mountain? Why didn't he stay on flat earth? Why did he climb it alone?[1]

Later, in reclaiming his son's body, the undertaker handed him his son's boots and backpack, clean and unscathed. Imagine the cruel mockery-you go to claim the bruised and battered body of your beloved son, and here are perfect shoes, an advertisement that says "You can fall down a mountain, and I will still maintain my looks, ready to be worn again by family and friends!"[2]

A lady in one of the grief classes that I taught lost her husband to a heart attack. She was angry at her husband for not having treated his heart pains more seriously. "He was so macho that he did not think he had to go to the doctor,even though I pleaded with him to do so." Earl Grollman writes,

> You are infuriated with your loved one for leaving you. The beloved is 'at rest' but you now have the weight of the world on your shoulders.[3]

Anger may also be directed at God or at religion in general. We often live life with the idea that if we believe in God, and obey His Word, then God will bless us by not allowing anything bad to happen to us. Problems may come to the lives of evil and mean-spirited individuals, but not to God's children. Nowhere does the Bible teach this idea, but many believe it anyway. Problems, whether they be pain, or cancer, or sudden death, come to God's children as well as to others. God does provide for His faithful the fortitude to deal with such problems, but He does not automatically take the problems away. The question of pain, suffering, and the problem of evil will be addressed in the next chapter.

Martha Bittle Clark wrote a book that dealt with her innermost feelings as she struggled with the car accident that took the life of her eighteen year old daughter, Sherry. In her book **Are You Weeping with me, God?**, she writes,

> My heart tells me that you do not cause accidents to happen, that they are man-made, not God-made...I would never accept a God who

chose to punish me, teach me a lesson, or make me a better person by taking the life of my child. I can hardly bear the anger of knowing you even allowed the accident to happen...[4]

ANGER.For a religious person, it sounds strange to suggest that a person can become angry. Perhaps anger is the wrong word. When we hear the word, the connotation of someone throwing a "temper tantrum" takes place. Anger might better be labeled hurt, frustration, fear, helplessness, or various other feelings. Whatever it is, it is an emotion, and emotion will be expressed in grief, whether others give us that right or not. It is suggested that people learn to express their feelings. Rather than directing anger at only one person, one might properly say, "I feel angry about..." or "I feel guilty about...."[5] You are saying, "This is how I feel. This expresses my thoughts at this time." By doing this, one shows that this is a phase that one must go through as one works through their grief. It is not an emotion that will hurt others or yourself, but it is a feeling of helplessness that is felt as one tries to readjust to a life that has been turned inside out because of death.[6]

Right now you are wounded-no explanation in the world will make that wound go away. You have a thousand whys-ask them all. You have a million feelings-feel them all. You have a billion hurts-and deserve everyone of them. For now feel what you feel.[7]

GUILT AND BITTERNESS

As one continues in what Rando calls the "confrontation phase," there will be guilt that must be dealt with. Guilt comes at you in various forms. There is guilt over what you said or did not say before the loved one died. There is guilt over action that was or was not acted upon. There is guilt in the fact that you are living and they have died. Any laughter or bright moment in your life might bring back a feeling of betrayal.[8]

Guilt is often expressed in two words—"if only." "If only I had...treated the one I loved more kindly. Called the doctor sooner. Understood the full extent of the illness. Taken better care of him or her. Not lost my temper. Expressed my affection more frequently."[9]

"If only" can become a nightmare for a griever, for there are never any acceptable answers to the queries it has. To make matters worse, the "if onlys" may be possibly correct. Maybe there were things you could have done that you did not do. Perhaps there were words that could have been spoken that were not spoken. Perhaps there were actions that could have been taken that were not. The fact is, we are all imperfect human beings. Hindsight may be twenty twenty, but we have to make decisions based on the information that we have available. As Earl Grollman writes, "What is past is past. It cannot be changed. You already have too much pain to add the burden of self-accusation, self-reproach, and self-depreciation."[10]

A member of the grief class that I taught had a husband who took his own life. She felt guilty for not "seeing what he was about to do." She was kindly told that she could not hold herself accountable for the decision that he made not to live. He was an adult and chose to make this decision. Although we would like to protect everyone from harm, the fact is that adults are free moral agents who can choose whether to live or die.

Yet, we have to realize that "if onlys" and guilt lead to a dead-end street. We can learn from our mistakes and we can improve on the future based on the past, but we cannot change what is already behind us. Guilt is a necessary phase that must be worked through.

READJUSTMENT AND ADAPTATION

Referred to as the accommodation phase, Rando suggests that in this phase there is a gradual decline of grief. Slowly you begin emotional and social reentry into the everyday world. Although the loss is not forgotten (it never will be), you begin to adjust to a new life without your beloved. The emotional investment that you gave to them now begins to be channeled in other directions or in other ways.[11]

Life has thrown you a curveball, and it has overwhelmed you. Now you begin to adjust to it, much like a person who learns to walk all over again, after the breaking of a leg. You decide that you will go on with your life, shattered though it may be. "Accommodation comes when you decide you care whether your life continues or not...I am going on with my life here, and I find joy in it."[12]

Sissy Thomas tells of the incident of the shooting death of her twenty-four-year-old son, Hugh. She told of her own death emotionally, and how that she did not care if life continued for her. She tells of the crossroads that she faced.

> Either, I could be absorbed deeper into my pit of self destruction and not be of any good to anyone or I could try to pull myself out. I made up my mind that the person who decided when, where and how my son would die was not going to have any more power over me or my family. He was not going to destroy what shreds of life we had left. I began to focus on how Hugh lived, not how he died.[13]

This is the attitude one manifests in the phase of adaptation and readjustment. You make the best of the situation, beginning to crawl out of the pit of grief, that you of necessity have been forced to be in for months.

Notice that to this point, nothing has been said about how long the grief journey takes. The reason is that no one can set that time duration for anyone. Other chapters have revealed reasons and influences that will bring forth longer grief journeys for some as opposed to others. Normally, textbooks have revealed that one's grief journey will take eighteen months to two years, but for some it will be longer. For others, perhaps because of advancing age or other circumstances, it may not take as long. Whatever the time, this phase of readjustment comes after the real pain has been felt and the work of grief has gone·on for a long time.

HOPE AND A NEW REALITY

"You have changed. You have grown. You understand for the first time what the Psalmist meant when he said, 'Yea, though I walk through the shadow of death.' The important words are WALK THROUGH. YOU WALK THROUGH. You do not remain where you were. Life is for the living."[14]

These words adequately sum up this final and ongoing transition into life again. You are still grieving and will continue to grieve at times of special remembrances (holidays, birthday of deceased, anniversaries, etc,), but now you see the light at the end of the tunnel. You have gone back to living and you have accepted life as it is.

You begin to make major decisions once again. You can look at mementos of your loved ones and remember good times together, via the tears. You can laugh and smile again even though the pain still comes back at times.[15] You have not forgotten the loss you have, but you have chosen to remain alive. Grief is not forgetting, but it is in discovering the essence of who and what the deceased person meant to you. Martha Bittle Clark found this at the end of her grief journey when she wrote,

> Every life affects someone or something!... The
> meaning of life is found, not so much in what
> we do, no matter how good that may be, but
> rather in how we affect or change the lives of
> others. And isn't that the purpose of it all,
> God? That our being here matters?[16]

In the movie, **To Dance with a White Dog,** an old
gentleman has to make it through life without his aged
wife by his side. At the end of the movie, as his children
are denying the impending death that will soon be his,
he bids them to remember this idea: "Remember, death
is not about endings—only discoveries!"

Grief does bring discovery, a discovery of what our
loved one was all about. Nicholas Wolterstorrff, in
remembering his son Eric, writes,

> All around us are his things: his clothes, his
> books, his camera, the things he made-pots,
> drawings, slides, photos, papers. They speak
> with forked tongue, words of joyful pride and
> words of sorrow. Do we put them all behind
> doors to muffle the sorrow or leave them out to
> hear them tell of the hands that shaped them?
> We shall leave them out... we will put them
> where they confront us. This as a remembrance,
> as a memorial.[17]

Another discovery that grief brings is in our thoughts
concerning God. Loss forces us to re-examine our beliefs
about God, goodness and evil, and a host of other complex
matters. When our faith becomes sifted through the loss
that we sustain, what "falls out" may be nice-sounding
statements that we thought were right but now realize
are not appropriate. What remains then is the real faith,
that rock-like substance that has carried us through our
grief journey, and will carry us through. God is there, and
He is still a "very present help in time of trouble," but

now we believe that statement in a way that was unknown to us on the other side of our grief journey.

> Sorrow has a refining influence on the soul, and it can help an individual put priorities in their proper perspective and clarify values...the individual who has a deep, abiding faith and trust in God comes through the experience stronger and is usually motivated to reach out to others going through similar tragedies.[18]

You see, a new you has been created. You are not, and never will be, the person you were before your loss. Grief has strengthened you and has made you more realistic and hopefully better. "Better" not in the sense that you are better off without your loved one-that can never be. But "better" because you now appreciate the loved one that you had, you better understand who and what they were, and you better understand that living involves the acceptance of loss. Because of your loss, you are now able to help others with their future losses. Because of your journey, the hope is that you can help others know of some of the "obstacles" they will encounter along the way. Helping others also brings therapeutic help to one's life as well. It also allows you to hold up and memorialize your loved one by doing things in their memory. Thankfully, "precious memories" can never be taken from us. As long as we live, we can keep our loved ones alive through such memories.

WORKS CITED

1   Nicholas Wolterstorff, **Lament for a Son**, (Grand Rapids: Wm. B. Eerdmans, 1987), p. 19.

2   Ibid, 17,18.

3   Earl A. Grollman, **Living When A Loved One has Died**, (Boston: Beacon Press,1977), p. 30.

4   Martha Bittle Clark, **Are You Weeping with Me,**

God?, (Nashville: Broadman Press, 1987), pp. 50,51.

5   Doug Manning, **Don't Take my Grief away from Me**, (Hereford, Texas: Insight Books, 1979), p. 71.

6   Therese A. Rando, **How to go on Living when Someone You love Dies**, (New York: Bantam Books, 1988), p. 22.

7   Manning, 50.

8   Rando, 21-23.

9   Grollman, Living, 39.

10   Ibid, 41.

11   Rando, 23.

12   Janice Harris Lord, **No Time for Goodbyes**, (Ventura, California: Pathfinder Publishing, 1987),p.31.

13   Used with Permission by Sissy Thomas in "From the Heart" in **The Compassionate Friends Newsletter**, Orlando, Florida, as seen in **The Compassionate Friends Newsletter**, Tuscaloosa, Alabama, May-June, 1995, p. 2.

14   Grollman, Living, 112,113.

15   Earl A. Grollman, Editor, **What Helped me when my Loved one Died**,(Boston: Beacon Press, 1981), pp. 149,150.

16   Clark, 108.

17   Wolterstorff, 28,29.

18   Kuenning, 257.

Chapter 6

Why Did God Let Them Die?

The Question Of Evil And The Goodness Of God

by Don Williams

When life is going smoothly as we think it should go, there are few if any questions concerning God and the reasons why things happen as they do. But when a baby dies, or a little child is killed in an accident, or a horrible accident takes place, ending the lives of many people, there are a great deal of people who want to know WHY. "Why did God let this happen; could He not have prevented this from happening?"

As I sit and write these words, it has been less than forty-eight hours since a TWA 747 jet crashed into the waters off of Long Island in New York. Although it has not yet been determined why the jet crashed, the great fear is that terrorists had something to do with this fiery accident, which claimed the lives of two hundred and thirty people. The question "why" has been asked many times so far, and will continue to be asked. If this was a terrorist group that caused the accident, why were they not discovered? "How could God allow innocent people to die" is a statement that will be asked anytime a terrible tragedy takes place.

The problem of evil and the goodness of God has been debated for several hundred years. In the Old Testament, when bad things happened in the life of Job, he wanted to question God as to why these things were happening to him. He soon found out that there was much more to the question than he could understand. He discovered that the marvels of this world and the complexities of nature were far greater than mortal man could ever understand.

At the same time, we are curious people, and when problems and heartaches come into our lives, we wonder why such tragedies and problems happen. The thinking goes like this: "If God is so powerful and mighty, then why do bad things happen to good people?" It is understood when bad things happen to wicked and evil people. We believe that is such instances, there is a connection between cause and effect, and rightly so.

But what about innocent babies who die of cancer or leukemia? What about babies who are born with defects? And why does it happen to some babies and not to others? Concerning unanswerable questions like these, Delores Kuenning writes,

> Is God punishing them? Does God have a plan so all-important that He intentionally causes the baby's death, the accident, the cancer?...Does God cause such things so that He can teach lessons that can be learned only through pain and suffering?[1]

Martha Bittle Clark, in writing her personal thoughts to God concerning her feelings after the death of her daughter wrote,

> Why would the Creator of all life wish harm to come to, not only my daughter, but any innocent child? Is it true, as some lady told me, that you have a plan for every life? Was there some great Master Plan that said Sherry Clark had to die on the fourth of July, and the friend, the rain, the curve in the road, and the tree all served as agents of this scheme to ensure that she met her destiny?[2]

When tragedy happens, it is easier to call God into account for what has happened, rather than explaining it in some other way. Such phrases as "it was God's will" or "God needed another angel" suggest this thought. Martha Bittle Clark tells of a lady who said she knew why Clark's daughter had died, and yet why her daughter, who had been in a car accident, had survived. "God knew I was not strong enough to handle something this terrible." Clark wrote,

> What irony if this is true. Do the weak pray to become strong so they can be brought to their
> • knees and made weak again? The very idea is obscene. I turn the shower off and know that I can never forgive you, God.[3]

We will now examine this complex problem, discussing the reasons for pain and suffering. An examination of how God operates and helps in the midst of pain and suffering will also be discussed.

WHY IS THERE PAIN AND SUFFERING?

There are several reasons why there is pain and heartache in our lives. Some pain and suffering come as the result of the choices we make. In the Garden of Eden, Adam and Eve made a choice to eat of the forbidden fruit, and mankind has been paying for their error and decision ever since. They also paid for it in having to leave the paradise life of Eden. Adam would have to work and sweat to make a living for his family, and Eve would have to endure the pain of childbirth. They would also eventually die, an appointment that all mankind must keep. In Romans 6:23, the Apostle Paul writes that "the wages of sin is death."

The consequences of the choices of mankind are seen in the destructive lives that some people lead. Every day, people die because of the consequences of their addictive lifestyle to alcohol, tobacco, drugs, and other self-destructing habits. It is sad to think that people could have lived longer if they had taken better care of themselves. We have heard the old adage, "if you play with fire, you will get burned." It is also the case that people sometimes choose to make a decision that will hasten and bring forth pain, suffering, and eventual death.

Some suffering and pain comes as a result of wrong decisions that others make. Everyday innocent people are killed in traffic accidents by drunk drivers who get behind the wheel of a vehicle and drive in such a way so as to cause the wreck. Imagine the one hundred and sixty plus families in Oklahoma who grieve today because of the diabolical plan of a few to blow up the federal courthouse building in Oklahoma City. These innocent men, women and children were going about their normal routine for the day, when all of the sudden the bomb went off, and their lives were snuffed out. The families of these innocent victims and our nation continue to pay the consequences of anguish and suffering to this day.

Jesus referred to such pain and suffering in Luke thirteen, when he tells of a tower that fell on eighteen men and killed them. Jesus argued that it was not their fault that such a tragedy took their lives. Ken Filkins, in his book, **Comfort Those who Mourn**, tells of a three year old riding her tricycle in the front yard of her home. A drunk driver came around the corner in a car, lost control of the car, and ran over the little girl, killing her. Someone, he said, trying to comfort the mother, told her "It was God's will." Filkins commented,

> How can it be God's will when no part of the equation was God's will? Was it God's will for the man to be drunk? Was it God's will for him to disobey the civil law about driving while

intoxicated? Was it God's will for him to break the speed limit? Was it God's will to...hit a child riding her tricycle? "No" to all the above.[4]

Sadly, much suffering takes place because of the wrongful choices that others make.

Some suffering and pain and death can come because of diseases, through no fault of the patient. We can see a cause and effect between alcohol and tobacco with those who have liver and lung problems. But what about those who develop liver and lung problems, and never pick up the bottle, or light up the first cigarette?

We live in a world that is imperfect, full of germs, viruses, and diseases. It may be that this is a result of the death that God pronounced upon man because of the sin in the Garden of Eden. Filkins likens these defects to the results of neglect of natural laws. At the same time, we cannot blame God for causing or even allowing such things as cancer, cholera, etc. Filkins tells of a man in India who lost his child to cholera, and blamed it on God, saying it was His will. A preacher told him the following story:

> Suppose someone crept up the steps into your veranda and deliberately put a wad of cotton soaked in cholera germ culture over your little girl's mouth. What would you think about that?" "Who would do such a thing?" the Indian asked. "Such a person should be killed. What do you mean by suggesting such a thing?" "Isn't that just what you have accused God of doing when you said it was His will? Call your child's death the result of mass ignorance, call it mass folly, call it mass sin. If you like, call it bad drains or communal carelessness, but don't call it the will of God.[5]

All four of my grandparents have died, two to cancer,

one of a heart attack, and one to tuberculosis. Our family never blamed God for their deaths. All lived good lives, living into their sixties, and one even reached the age of eighty. I do not know why they had the diseases they did, but to point a finger at God and say He is to blame is unethical, and perhaps even immoral. As Martha Bittle Clark writes,

> We may never know why one child gets a new bicycle and another gets leukemia. Or why one person escapes a car accident without a scratch and another one dies. Or even why there is so much sadness in some lives and almost none in others....[6]

Some suffering and death and destruction comes through violation of the laws of nature. Fire can be used for heating, cooking, warming, and other good purposes. A fire out of control can cause great destruction, and even death. High winds, floods, and earthquakes can also cause great destruction. Why are there such destructive forces in our world today?

God, in creating this world, placed laws of natural force and gravity into motion. They were set in place for the purpose of keeping God's world orderly and in motion. Rain and wind are good forces, in that they bring necessary moisture for crops and drive smog and other pollutants away. However, when mixed with atmospheric pressures, they can cause tornadoes and hurricanes which bring forth probable destruction. I once lived in a town where a tornado struck, killing thirteen people. Was it "their time to go," so that they would die in such a sudden and tragic way? Of course not—it is a cold fact of reality that when forces of nature meet with corruptible, perishable materials such as buildings, homes, trailers and cars, there will often be destruction.

Why does God allow such destructive laws of nature

to exist? Why does He allow earthquakes, typhoons, tornadoes, etc.? Why would He allow roads to be made slippery through ice and snow, so that folks would slide on them in their cars, causing wrecks and sometimes death? Perhaps I can illustrate the problem in this way.

I am a avid Alabama fan, and especially love Alabama football. Our great rivals in college football are Auburn and Tennessee. Let's suppose that we are playing Auburn, and we are mounting a final drive to beat them. Our quarterback throws a pass into the extreme corner of the end zone, and the receiver catches the ball with one foot in bounds, just inches from the out of bound line. The referee signals a touchdown, and we go ahead by five points. Auburn now gets the ball, and with time running out, begins to march the ball upfield. Their quarterback throws a "hail Mary" pass into the extreme corner of the end zone, and their receiver catches the ball, with one foot inside the boundaries by just a few inches. However, the referee waves the play off, saying that he had to have both feet inside the out of bounds marker, and not just one foot. Chaos would take place, and rightly so. The reason—the rules were not the same for one team as for another.

If God worked in such a way, so that He saved this car as it was about to slide off the road and over a cliff, and He did not do the same for you if you were in a similar situation, that would make Him a respector of persons. It would also compromise His laws of force and energy. If He saved one town from the destructive path of a coming tornado, then to be consistent, He would have to do the same thing for a small town on the other side of the world, about to swept away by a monsoon. How can God be God, if He is always superseding His own laws that were set into motion at creation?

Again, all laws of nature are not exclusively evil.

Monsoons and tornadoes bring necessary rain and moisture that are needed to make crops grow. God has chosen to abide by the laws of nature that have been set into motion. Filkins writes,

> Some say that God could stop suffering by programming nature (or. individuals) never to do evil. For instance, God could program automobiles to do good...but not to do evil (robbing banks, kidnapping, or allowing drunk driving). But allowing freedom means risking the abuse of that freedom. That abuse-sin-is not desired by God, nor is it his will.[7]

IS THERE ANY VALUE TO PAIN AND SUFFERING?

Discussing the subject of evil causes one to wonder if there is any value to pain at all. The answer is yes. Although pain can bring eventual death to beloved others, there is some value to pain and suffering.

First of all, pain warns us that something is wrong. A person may begin to experience numbness in his arm and shoulder. He may begin to experience shortness of breath, or pain in his chest. These signs may be a prelude to an approaching heart attack, and by checking these pains out immediately by going to a doctor or to the hospital, future pains and possible death may be avoided. Pain is not always bad. Pain can be a warning that something is wrong, and that one needs immediate attention.

Pain and suffering force us to look to God in times of need. If we were self-sufficient, totally in control of our lives as human beings, we might feel that we would never need the help of a higher Being. Yet, as great as the wonders and marvels of science and medicine are today (thanks to the providence of God), science and medicine can only go so far. There is only so much that mortal man can do to alleviate pain and suffering. We need the Almighty Father in our lives, the "God of mercies, and the God of all comfort" (2 Corinthians 1:3). He can be "our refuge and strength, a very present help in trouble" (Psalm 46:1). John Claypool, in commenting on the part religion played in his life after the death of his daughter, wrote,

> I am now willing to affirm that the Ground
> which sustained me then is still firm enough to
> • support the weight of life. I am more convinced
> than ever that the hope of biblical religion is
> authentic vision and realistic perspective.[0]

Pain and suffering allow us to receive help from others. As Paul writes in Romans 14:7, "For none of us liveth to himself, and no man dieth to himself." How sad if we could never be allowed to show our compassion and concern for others. This is what Jesus did repeatedly in His life, and it is this "mind" (Philippians 2:3-5) that is to be in the lives of His followers. It is often in helping others that we find the greatest help for ourselves. Countless books suggest that administering care to others is tremendous therapy for "surviving grievers" who are working through their own loss and problems. As Helen Keller once said, "As long as you sweeten another's pain, life is not in vain."[9]

A final value of pain and suffering is that it causes us to long for, and earnestly live for the place of heaven. If this life was without problems, heartaches, pain and sorrows, why would we desire to leave it and go to another place? Yet, God has described heaven as a place worth living for. In Revelation 21:4, John records these words: "And God shall wipe away all tears from their eyes; and there shall be no more death, neither sorrow nor crying, neither shall be any more pain–for the former things are passed away." It will be a place of great happiness, as we are re-united with faithful loved ones who have already died. The best of all people of all time will be there as well. And to think-we will live in the presence of Almighty God, His son Jesus, and the Holy Spirit. Indeed, heaven will surely be worth it all, including the pain we must deal with here below!

DOES GOD CARE WHEN I SUFFER?

Where is God when suffering comes our way? Does He know what is happening to us? Does He even care? Is it our fault when pain and suffering comes our way?

These are questions that will be asked when a tragedy comes our way. A man in the first grief class that I taught had lost his wife to cancer. He wrote this question for discussion in the class: "Someone made the comment to me that 'anyone can be healed; there is no limit on God's power, only on the vessel'...I know many people who prayed and had faith. I prayed for one and a half years and my wife had as much faith as anyone I know. I was made to feel as if we lacked something in our faith..."

Is God concerned about my suffering, and about yours? The Bible responds with a definite YES. When God's son Jesus is introduced to us in scripture, He is referred to as a man of sorrows. Isaiah 53:7 refers to Him as "a man of sorrows and acquainted with grief." When Jesus came to this earth, He was not made in a body different than our own. John 1:14 tells us that He was made flesh and He lived among us. He was made with all the emotions that we experience in life. Jesus, in His short time upon earth, would experience tiredness, anger, hunger, thirst, tears, and the frustration and pain that death brings. In the narrative of the death of His friend Lazarus, the text reveals that "when Jesus therefore saw her weeping, and the Jews also weeping which came with her, he groaned in the spirit, and was troubled." "Jesus wept" as He reacted to the pain and suffering that Mary and Martha felt over the loss of their brother" (John 11:33,35).

Upon the cross, Jesus asked a question that we are prone to ask today when unexpected heartaches come our way–WHY? His words to God were, "My God, My God, why hast thou forsaken me?" (Matthew 27:46) What was meant by this statement? As the Son of God, Jesus knew that a perfect, sinless sacrifice was the only thing that could atone for man's sins. Thus, Deity would have to give Himself for the sins of man. At the same time, He, as the Son of Man, must have been echoing the sentiments that mortal man feel when things happen that we do not understand. The question which Jesus asked was also asked by Job and Gideon in the Old Testament. It is a question that we ask today.

Notice, if you will, that Jesus's final statement was one of committal to God. His questioning did not deter Him from placing his life into the trust and hands of God. In Luke 23:46, the doctor Luke records those final words: "Father, into thy hands I commend my spirit: and having said thus, he gave up the ghost." We would do well to commit our lives to God, regardless of the questions we have. Deuteronomy 29:29 suggest that there are "secret things" that belong only to God.

After Jesus died, He was placed in the tomb, and three days later was raised from the dead. He is then introduced to mankind as the wounded Son of Man. Do you remember that in John 20, when Jesus appears to His ten disciples in the room where they were hidden, that He showed them the wounds upon His body? He showed to them the effects of the spikes within His hand, and the spear that was thrust in His side. Why were they there? Could the God that brought Him forth from the dead not also have given Him a perfect body, one with no scars or blemishes?

Dr. Paul Brand's specialty in medicine is the hand. In contemplating God's pain on the cross, he asked:

> Why did Christ keep the scars? He could have had a perfect body, or no body, when he returned in splendor in heaven. Instead he carried with him remembrances of his visit to earth. For a reminder of His time here, He chose scars. That is why I say God hears and understands our pain, and even absorbs it into Himself—because He kept those scars as a lasting image of wounded humanity. He has been here; He has borne the sentence. The pain of man has become the pain of God.[10]

What a wonderful reminder of God's love for us! God does care, and He shows that care by keeping intact in His Son's body the scars given to Him because of sin. The sin of others caused Jesus to die. My sins and your sins put Him on the cross as well. Yet He kept the scars, as He went back to heaven. And He cried tears in John 11, when a human being who He loved died, even though He would soon raise him from the dead. My friends, if Deity (Jesus) could feel pain with the loss of His beloved friend, then He (as well as God) must be pained with our losses. We sing the song and ask the question, "Does Jesus care when my heart is pained, too lonely for mirth and song..." The answer is rightly found in the chorus: "Oh yes, He cares, I know He cares, His heart is touched with my grief."

It is gratifying to know that we have a Savior who has been "touched with the feelings of our infirmities"

(Hebrews 4:15) The promise from a God who does not lie is that if we serve Him faithfully, He has promised not "to leave us, nor forsake us" (Hebrews 13:5). Even though there are many unanswered questions about pain and suffering that we will never understand, there is a God above who does care about us, and will help us to deal with our pain and suffering. Martha Bittle Clark, in her book, concludes,

> God's will for the world is good, not evil, I wanted to say. It isn't ugliness, but beauty. And it certainly isn't tragic accidents for our precious children, but long productive lives lived in his service and for his glory...what God wants for our lives is good, but what we choose is not always good. The whole scheme of life has been designed around freedom of choice, the greatest gift of love ever given to a created being.[11]

The issue becomes what will we do with our choice of life? Will we use it for self, selfishly blaming others for anything that does not happen right within our lives? Or will we use our lives as Jesus would desire, seeking to help others and showing our compassion for wounded people like ourselves? As Randy Becton, who endured several bouts of lymphoma cancer wrote,

> Human need rarely comes when it is convenient. The cries of suffering people will always interrupt our peaceful lives. The issue is, who are we? Are we suffering servants of the Suffering servant?...We always have to choose to suffer along with others.[12]

WORKS CITED

1   Delores Kuenning, **Helping People Through Grief**, (Minneapolis: Bethany House, 1987), p. 20.
2   Martha Bittle Clark, **Are You Weeping with me,**

God?, (Nashville: Broadman Press, 1987), p. 30.

3   Ibid, 30. ·

4   Kenn Filkins, **Comfort Those who Mourn**, (Joplin, Missouri: College Press Publishing, 1992), p. 131.

5   Ibid, 132,133.

6   Clark, 71.

7   Filkins, 127,128.

8   John Claypool, **Tracks of a Fellow Struggler**, (Waco, Texas: Word Publishing, 1974), p. 15.

9   Warren Wiersbe, comp., **Classic Sermons on Suffering**, (Grand Rapids: Kregel, 1984), p. 125.

10   Dr. Paul Brand and Philip Yancey, **In His Image,** (Grand Rapids: Zondervan Publishing House, 1984), p. 291.

11   Clark, 99.

12   Randy Becton, **Does God Care when We Suffer?**, (Grand Rapids: Baker Book House, 1988), p. 95.

Chapter 7

Why Doesn't The Bible Help Me?
The Bible And The Subject Of Grief

by Ron Williams

D eath comes uninvited, knocking at our door, and destroying our lives by the loss of someone that we love. Often, death comes when we least expect it. It can come with our knowledge that it is going to occur. Either way, it comes without our blessings....without our permission ....inspite of our pleas and our prayers, death comes and turns our world upside down!

When such happens, we wonder, where do we turn for help? As a minister of the gospel of Christ, I would suggest that the obvious place to turn would be the Word of God, the Bible. Unfortunately, many individuals make the mistake of thinking that the Bible cannot be relevant to the problems of today. Because the Bible is several thousand years old, they believe that such an ancient book cannot be useful and practical to deal with the trauma and pain of grief. Such is not the case with the timeless and ageless thoughts of God that were written down by men who were "moved with the Holy Spirit" to write down those words (2 Peter 1:20-21).

From the beginning of God's relationship with mankind in the Garden of Eden in Genesis one, to the end of time with the promise of God's people to be in heaven in Revelation twenty-two, the subject of life and death are explored completely in the Bible. No stone is left unturned in regard to a full discussion of grief being found in God's Word.

For example, the word grief is found some twenty-four times in the Old Testament and two times in the New Testament. The word grieve is found seven times in the Old Testament and also two times in the New Testament as well. The word grieved is found on some thirty occasions in the Old Testament while the word occurs some seven times in the New Testament.

EXAMPLES OF GRIEF IN THE BIBLE

Time and space will not permit us to look at every occasion where the subject of grief is discussed in God's Word. Notice the following four examples of how grief is portrayed in the Bible.

In Genesis 26: 34-35, we read of the grief that Isaac and Rebekah had over the marriage of their son, Esau. The text reads, "When Esau was forty years old, he took as wives Judith the daughter of Beeri the Hittite, and Basemath the daughter of Elon the Hitite. And they were a grief of mind to Isaac and Rebekah." You may remember that in our first chapter that we made the point that grief can be a result of many kinds of losses. Please notice that Isaac and Rebekah were grieved–not because Esau was dead, but because he had married two women outside the family lineage of Abraham! Isaac and Rebekah, understanding the possible problems that could come from marrying someone of another ethnic lineage of that time period, were grieved in mind for what could happen to their son!

In 1 Samuel one, we have the narrative of a woman named Hannah that was praying to God in the tabernacle at Shiloh. As she is praying to herself, Eli, the priest, thinks she is drunk and chastises her for her supposed drunkenness. Hannah explains that she is not drunk as he thinks, but she is a woman that is pouring out her heart to God. In verse 16 of that chapter, she explains, "Do not consider your maidservant a wicked woman, for out of the abundance of my complaint and grief I have spoken until now."

If one will read the remainder of 1 Samuel one they will begin to understand what kind of grief that Hannah was expressing. Hannah was one of two wives married to a man named Elkanah. Elkanah's other wife, Peninnah, had several children by her husband, but Hannah's womb was barren and she had not been able to have children. Not only was Hannah experiencing the grief that comes from the lack of biological children, but her husband's other wife provoked Hannah and chided her for her barrenness.

As Hannah was praying to God, she was praying as a woman that was consumed with the grief that came from not being able to bring children into the world. In a world today where many couples have difficulty in having children, surely one could understand the great amount of grief that she felt!

In Second Chronicles 6:28-29, we find the author discussing another kind of grief that people had to deal with then as well as today. The text reads,

> When there is famine in the land, pestilence or blight or mildew, locusts or grasshoppers; when their enemies besiege them in the land of their cities; whatever plague or whatever sickness there is; whatever prayer, whatever supplication is made by anyone, or by all Your people Israel, when each one knows his own burden and his own grief, and spreads out his hands to this temple:

No doubt all landowners know of the terrible misfortune

that is felt when their land is destroyed by elements of disease and nature. The writer here laments these tragedies that occur and state that these are a source of grief to individuals that lose their land and possible income to such disasters.

The Book of Job, in its entirety, deals with the subject of grief that is caused by a multitude of problems of life. In Job 6:2-3, Job says, "Oh, that my grief were fully weighed, and my calamity laid with it on the scales! For then it would be heavier than the sand of the sea-therefore my words have been rash." If ever there was a man that was besieged with grief, it would have to be the man named Job! As the first few chapters of his book reveal, Job grieved due to many cumulative losses in his life. In what appears to be but a matter of moments, Job loses his household servants, his ten children, his wealth, his health, all of his crops, and even the support of his wife. It is no wonder that Job states that if his grief was weighed, it would weigh more than even the sand of the sea!

In examining these four examples of how grief is discussed in the Bible, one will notice that each incident deals with a different kind of grief. As we have said before, it is a mistake to think that grief is caused ONLY by the death of a loved one. Each of these cases deal with other kinds of losses besides the obvious grief that is felt when a loved one dies. Such grief as an anguish of feelings over the marriage plans of one's children, the despair that comes from being unable to have children, and the grief that comes from calamities of nature, are all real sources of grief for people for any time period of history. The Bible is quite up-to-date on situations of life that occur frequently today that are a source of real grief to individuals involved in such problems.

RITUALS OF GRIEVING IN THE BIBLE

The Bible not only deals with various forms of grieving, but also describes the manner in which people grieved as well. When God's leader, Moses died, the people mourned and wept due to his death for thirty days (Deuteronomy 34:8). Job's three friends, when they heard of the many losses that had occurred to him, traveled to him and sat silent with him for seven days without saying a word (Job 2:11-13). When the prophet Ezekiel was sent by God to the Judean captives in Babylon, he came to Tel Abib and sat there with them for a period of seven days before he spoke a single word (Ezekiel 3:15). In John's narrative of the death of Jesus's friend, Lazarus, John records how Jesus felt about his friend's death when he wrote, "Jesus wept" (John 11:35). When the Apostle Paul wrote to the church in Rome, he reminded them that one of a christian's duties was to "rejoice with those that rejoice and weep with those that weep" (Romans 12:15).

These various scriptures suggest three important factors that were important to people in the Bible concerning their grieving rituals. Notice that ample time was given to the people in regard to their mourning for Moses (Deuteronomy 34:8). Such is a must for all people if they ever want to get through their grieving for someone that they loved. Notice as well the importance of friends that came to be with the grieving person(s) in regard to their grief (Job 2:11-13, Ezekiel 3:15). Real friends understand the value of being there for the grieving person without having to say a word. Finally, John 11:35 and Romans 12:15 suggest the importance of caregivers being real and genuine with their own feelings of grief. It is so comforting to know that Christ was one that was willing to show His grief concerning the death of His friend. When a person grieves, they should not be ashamed to express how they feel about their grief. These three factors are a must for anyone that wants to successfully work through their grief.

FUNERAL CUSTOMS IN THE BIBLE

The Bible is filled with example after example of individuals that died and were buried by their loved ones. One of the most interesting narratives of a funeral in the Bible is the death of Lazarus, the brother of Martha and Mary of Bethany. In John chapter eleven, we have an excellent depiction of what people of the First Century did in regard to their customs surrounding the death of a person. Notice some of these customs that are found in this chapter concerning the death of Lazarus.

Notice that when a person died, the family would soon thereafter bury the person out of their sight (John 11:17). Although it had been four days after the funeral of Lazarus, John 11:19 tells us that there were individuals that were with the grieving sisters to comfort them. These individuals were with Martha and Mary, both at their home in Bethany, and also accompanied them to the cave where their brother was buried as well (John 11:31).

Although these rituals seem common-place at first sight, it is interesting to note that these customs of the First Century are very similar to the customs that we practice in the Twentieth Century! When a death occurred, the family hurt and cried and suffered due to the lost of their loved one. When a death occurred, the family and friends gathered together and mourned the loss of that individual. With the loved one buried, the family cried for the loved one at home and also visited the grave of the loved one to mourn there as well. Caregivers visited the family after the funeral at their home and others accompanied the family to the grave as well. Even four days after the burial of the loved one, caregivers were still present to be with and to mourn with the family. Should it surprise us at all that many of the funeral customs that we practice today are found in the cultural traditions of people of the Bible?

GRIEF AND RELIGIOUS FAITH

Do religious people sin against God when they struggle with the emotion of grief in their lives? Is God angry at us when we falter and grope in darkness when we are besieged with the feelings of grief on every side? Does God expect more of us in our grieving than He does of the non-believer? Is it wrong for a religious person to grieve when their loved one dies?

These questions and others akin to them are often asked of people when they have suffered the loss of a loved one and they find themselves deep down in the pit of grief. They wonder if they are expressing a doubt in God, or if they are losing their faith, when they find themselves "as weak as water" in regard to their expressions of grief.

People that find themselves in such a dilemma as I have described need to be told that they are being human in regard to their feelings of grief. Just because a person is religious and maintains a faith in God does not mean that they will escape any suffering in this world. Although I firmly believe that an obedient faithful person has advantages over the non-believer in God in regard to their grieving, it does not take away any of the pain that they will suffer due to the loss of their loved one. Caregivers can do tremendous harm to the grieving person when we suggest that IF they would be more faithful to God these sufferings would not happen! Such a statement is preposterous and is totally contrary to the ideals that are expressed in God's Word.

When the Apostle Paul wrote to the church that met in Thessalonica, he was writing to christians that were enduring the loss of loved ones in death. Although these individuals were no doubt good people, they were, nevertheless, having to endure the reality that their loved ones were dying. Due to the fact that these brethren had a misconception concerning the second coming of Christ, these grieving individuals were very sorrowful. These grieving people believed that, due to the fact that their loved ones had died, that meant that there would be no hope for them to go to heaven to be with Christ. They mistakenly believed that one had to be alive if they wanted to be with the Lord in heaven.

As Paul is writing to them to straighten up this misunderstanding, he writes, "But I do not want you to be ignorant, brethren, concerning those who have fallen asleep, lest you sorrow as others who have no hope" (1 Thessalonians 4:13). Paul goes on to explain that God had the power to raise up these brethren who have died and would, in fact, raise them up first at the end of time (1 Thessalonians 4:16). Please notice, that as the apostle dealt with this problem, he does not chastise them for grieving for their loved ones. He does not condemn these christian brethren for their lack of faith in God by their sorrowful emotions of grief. Paul understood that it was natural and normal and healthy for these christian brethren to mourn and to sorrow for the loss of their loved ones in death. The only thing that he wanted them to do was to realize, that in their sorrowing, not to sorrow as those non-believers that had no hope in the afterlife!

In other words, the Apostle Paul was saying, "when your loved one dies, then you sorrow, you grieve, cry if you want to, be normal in your grieving process." Only remember, Paul wrote, that as you sorrow and grieve for that loved one, remember what Christ can do and don't sorrow like those people that have no hope in the afterlife."

This teaching, I believe, is the Bible's principle

concerning the relationship of our religious faith and the reality of death in our lives. There are times when our loss is so great, that we wonder if we can make it. Like the Apostle Paul and the church at Thessalonica, we need to remember to be normal and to allow ourselves to grieve for the great loss that we have suffered. In that grieving, however, let us not forget the promises of God for those individuals that have maintained a faithfulness of obedience to His Word. As Paul ended that particular chapter, he wrote, "Therefore comfort one another with these words," (1 Thessalonians 4:18). AMEN and AMEN!

Chapter 8

Where Are My Friends When I Need Them?
Why People Often Say And Do The Wrong Things

by Don Williams

In the movie **The Oldest Living Confederate Daughter**, the young mother and older Confederate husband have lost a two-year old child. The couple has five other children, but still the mother grieves over the loss of "Little Archie." The movie depicts the mother stationed in her bedroom, eating "starch" and refusing to come out. The children are forced to prepare food for themselves.

The grieving mother's parents come by to cheer her up. The mother talks about other deaths in the community and then tells her daughter that since it has been a month since the death of Archie, she needs to get up from her grief bed "and not wallow in it, but instead go on with your life." She finally leaves after hinting that if she does not get up and go on, her husband will not continue to love her, and their marriage will be over.

This video clip is often shown to grief support classes, and it is most interesting to hear (and see) their reactions. Some of them suggest that they have heard similar comments. Others say they would like to slap someone who would be so insensitive. Still others tell of how family members are often the ones who say the worst things.

Why is it that people often say and do the wrong things? There are various reasons. First of all, many people do not understand grief. A midwestern newspaper ran a man-on-the-street survey which asked people how long they thought it took to mourn the loss of a loved one. The answers given ranged anywhere from forty-eight hours to two weeks to six months. Answers like these show that many people do not have a concept of the all-encompassing nature of grief. As Doug Manning writes,

> When your grief extends beyond a few weeks, they begin to think you should be well by this time. When you do not get well, they begin to think you are odd in some way.[1]

Second, the majority of people who will come to comfort those who have lost a loved one have not experienced a significant loss of their own. Statistically, only 15% to 20% of people who come to visit with the grieving family have suffered the loss of a close relative. Therefore, when they come, they do not know what to say but feel like they have to say something. Being creatures of habit, they will repeat what they have heard others say in similar situations with similar losses.[2] The most frequent statement uttered is the phrase "I know how you feel." Delores Kuenning, in commenting on this oft-made statement writes, "Each person's grief is unique and no one can totally understand another's grief."[3] It is not possible to know how another person is feeling, since it is not possible of getting inside another person's body and mind.

Let's suppose that two neighbors lose their mothers in a similar type car wreck. The mothers and neighbors may be the same age. Still, there will be differences in the way they grieve. One neighbor may be single and her mother may have been a mainstay in her life. The other neighbor might be married with a family to support her in her loss. One neighbor's mother may have lived two blocks away, while the other neighbor's mother may have lived a thousand miles away, and was visited only rarely. Even if the mothers and daughter had many similar characteristics, still each had a different relationship. Other examples could be given, but suffice it to say, the phrase "I know how you feel" is not a proper statement made to grieving people.

Third, people often say and do the wrong thing because they are afraid of showing their own feelings. We hear early in life that "big boys and girls don't cry." Many think this is the way to react to death and loss and so they will suggest this idea of "no emotion" to those who have lost a loved one. Such phrases as "get a hold of yourself" or "keep a stiff upper lip" or "you have to be strong for your children" represent similar advice. They do this so they themselves will not break down and cry or express their feelings in a way that some would think is a sign of weakness.[4] "Friends usually get together and share ideas. Rarely do they get together and share feelings. Some people just cannot be around feelings. They are not only uncomfortable with yours, they are uncomfortable with their own."[5]

Fourth, people often say and do the wrong things in grief because death makes them uncomfortable. It is a fact that every day over five thousand Americans die. Yet, until it happens to someone that we know, or to a close relative, we are largely unaffected. When death comes to someone that is known, our lack of "comfort zone" for death causes us to talk about what is normally discussed everyday: the weather, sports, politics, our family, our aches and pains–everything but the pain and loss the grieving family is going through!

Fifth, people often say and do the wrong thing because we live in a "teller" society. Someone has suggested that since God gave man two ears and one tongue, one should listen twice as much as one speaks.

Yet, when someone tells of their problems, some think an answer must be given them. Manning writes, "The frustration of having no answer can cause us to either give shallow answers or just run from the question."[6] Often people will ramble on and on, using cliches they have heard others say, or give advice that is not needed.

Finally, people sometimes say and do the wrong thing because they try to "intellectualize" the feelings people have about grief. Informal surveys show four out of five reactions that grieving people hear following the loss of a loved one will imply that they *should not* be feeling the emotions they are feeling. Such phrases as "You should not feel that way" or "You should get on with your life" do nothing but complicate the grieving process, and place greater burdens upon the grieving family.[7]

No one has the right to tell grieving people how they should or should not feel. Reminding them of all the blessings they have had in the past is not relevant. Martha Bittle Clark tells a woman who reminded her that with her loss, she had other living children for which to be grateful. She writes,

> I wanted all of my children. I love them very much, but right now the resentment over what I don't have gets in the way of being grateful for what I do have. How could I possibly be thankful for the lives of my other children when this same life has been so cruelly snatched away from Sherry?[8]

Another mistake is to minimize the loss of a baby by suggesting to parents that they can always have other children. This is not only insensitive but it can also cause great hurt and further sorrow to the grieving parents. "Parents experience the death of their dreams and hopes for the future embodied in their wished-for baby. The age makes little difference; their pain is just as great."[9]

GRIEF AND STATEMENTS OF SPIRITUALITY

"Close friends come to sit with me because they know I need their love and support. Other friends are like Job's friends, telling me their personal philosophy of why such a tragedy had to happen."

"You are being tested," a portly woman declared as she sank into the cushions of my sofa yesterday.

"For what?" I quiried, "Isn't God omniscient? Doesn't He know me?"

"To see how strong your faith is," she nodded knowingly, "or to teach you something."

"You horrid old woman," I thought to myself. "What makes you think you know the mind of God.?[10]

This was Martha Bittle Clark's reaction to comments concerning the death of her eighteen year old daughter. The lady was suggesting that her daughter's death was attributed to God.

Although a previous chapter has dealt with suffering and the will of God, it is most interesting to think about statements that are made to grieving individuals concerning why the death occurred. "It must have been God's will" or "God took him/her" or "God must have needed another angel" are all too-common statements. Mary-Jane Creel writes,

I just hated to be told my daughter's illness and death were God's will. It made me feel as if God had betrayed me. Parents need to be supported by God, not betrayed by Him. I believe God allows these tragedies to be a part of our lives, but I certainly do not feel He wills such pain. It is best to keep such callous statements to yourself.[11]

Why do people suggest someone's death is the will of God? Sudden and unexpected death naturally raises many questions as to why loved ones died. Survivors will want to know what exactly happened to cause the death. They will want to know the cause of the death and the reason for the death. Well meaning people often suggests that such questions cannot be answered, and that God alone knows the answers. "Such a person implies that a mystical reason was responsible for your loved one's death, but the reason was known only to God. They imply that the reason is beyond understanding."[12] Such words only complicate the grief process. As Clark writes,

> Pious platitudes and biblical explanations have never done anything to help my sorrow. I secretly think such talk is easy as long as the death you are trying to explain is in someone else's family.[13]

As stated elsewhere, christians do not love or worship a God who intentionally takes the lives of loved ones. No one should attribute a death to an direct act of God. Why would God need a little child more than the parents? Or why would God need a thirty-five-year-old mother more than her children do at this time in their lives?

Instead of suggesting that one's death should be attributed to God, why not say "One comfort I find is that God has promised us that he will never leave us." This suggests to the griever that God does care in times of suffering and loss. One would do well to be careful in what is said to others. Attempts to try and "play God" should be avoided, as it is not possible for finite man to know the complete thoughts of an infinite God.

HELPFUL STATEMENTS TO SAY

Often in visiting with the grieving family, one is at a loss for words. Some stay away from grieving people for this reason. This makes their loss even harder to bear, because there is no one to express support and comfort. Words are important, for they aid in allowing the grieving family to know that they, as well as the loved one that died, are loved and remembered.

Sometimes these feelings are expressed in ways other than words. An elder told of the death of his father, a farmer all his life. Hundreds of people came to express their love and sympathy over the passing of this good man. As the elder put it, "Of all the people that came that night to the funeral home, I do not remember what anyone said except one old farmer. He came up to me, took my hand, and with tears streaming down his face said, 'I am so sorry.' "His words were the only ones I remember."

The following are some general statements that might be stated to members of a grieving family. The various statements would need to be used in a selective manner, based upon the loss and the nature of the loss.

"I am so sorry to hear about your loss."

"I can't imagine how painful this must be for you. I am so sorry."

" I am praying for you and I want you to know that I love you."[14]

Rather than saying "At least he doesn't have to suffer anymore" say "He suffered through alot, didn't he?"

Rather than saying "She wouldn't want you to grieve" say "It is difficult to say goodbye, isn't it?"

Rather than saying, "Call me if you need me." say to them "I want you to know that it is okay for you to be yourself around me. When you want to talk, I will be glad to listen."

Mary-Jane Creel, in her book **A Little Death**, includes a list of proper statements that can be made to bereaved parents in the loss of a baby or small child. She writes,

> How you say something means everything in conveying your condolences. First of all, present your feelings with depth, sincerity, strength, and meaning. Do not say it halfheartedly; do not act preoccupied with other things; do not act cheery, as though you were at a social event; and do not act rushed, as though you really do not have the time for their loss.[15]

She suggests the following statements as worthy of consideration:

"I care for what you are going through and what you will go through." This statement implies that one has given thought to the depth of the parents' loss. It also suggests that one realizes the future will be affected by the baby's death.

"I just wanted you to know I am thinking of you." "This remark lets the parents know you will not forget their loss as soon as you leave the room. It makes them feel good to know that you consider them in your thoughts."[16]

"I do not know what to say or do. I just wanted you to know I care for you." This shows to the grieving family that even though others feel awkward, they still care enough to come and acknowledge the loss the family is facing.[17]

"I will continue to pray for you." "This remark implies you have been praying for the parents, and you will keep praying for them, even after the funeral is over. This makes the parents feel that you will not forget about them after everything settles down. They need to know you realize it is not over after the funeral."[18]

All of these suggestions, followed by a hug or the touch of a hand, can be of great comfort. Grieving people need human strokes of affirmation and encouragement in time of grief. Words and touching can be great therapy.

HELPFUL THINGS THAT CAN BE DONE

There is nothing that can take the place of one's presence. When a death occurs, one should respond by going to be with the grieving family immediately, if possible. Almost thirty years ago, my grand-father died somewhat unexpectedly late one night. I remember some of our best friends coming over to the house and helping us get packed. This act of kindness has impressed me even unto this day.

There are occasions when distance and time will not allow one to visit or be present at a funeral. If this is the case, then flowers or some memorial sent in the name of the deceased is always appreciated. A phone call to acknowledge the loss is also appropriate. This allows the bereaved to know that you are thinking of them, even though you are not able to be there in person.

When a loved one dies, not only is it appropriate for one to go and visit the bereaved family, it is also helpful when various forms of help are offered. If the death was sudden, the phone will be ringing constantly. One can be of great help in answering the phone, or in making phone calls to relatives and friends (if the bereaved family so desires). Offers of transportation needs can be extended. Are there relatives that need to be picked up at the airport or bus station? Are there clothes that can be taken or picked up at the cleaners? Are there other errands that need to be taken care of at this time? One might volunteer to help in these various capacities.

If there are little children that are a part of the

grieving family, it might be a big help to offer to watch or baby-sit them at certain times. One can only imagine how hard it might be to meet friends and relatives at a funeral home with a two or three year old running around, holding on to the mother, etc. An offer to keep the children for a few hours might be of inestimable value.

Ladies from the church can be a great help by providing or serving food for a family during the time of the funeral. Ladies can be helpful in receiving food as it is brought. In some cases, food brought a few weeks after the funeral might be helpful, especially in the case of a traumatic loss.

Visits to the bereaved family are important, especially after the funeral. Ministers and friends might call first before they go, but normally visits a week after the funeral are appreciated. In some cases, grieving individuals need the presence of caring friends more after the funeral than before it. A visit every two weeks to one month in the first several months after the loss might be appropriate. Perhaps a phone call to the bereaved letting them know they are being thought of would be helpful. The number of visits one would make would depend upon one's relationship with the griever, the nature of the loss, and their reception to the visits that are made. One needs to remember that each person's grief is different.

It is also appropriate to remember special events like the birthday of the deceased, birthday of the loss, anniversary dates, holidays, etc. On days like these, a visit, call or card letting the grievers know that they are being thought of will normally be greatly appreciated. To let people know that they are being remembered in prayer on special days like these can bring great comfort.

A final way of helping the bereaved is written memorials in memory of their deceased. Sharing your special memories of their loved one will become treasures to the bereaved family. Other memorials–a tree planted in their memory, a book placed in the library in their memory, a candle lit at a memorial service in their memory–these are ways of acknowledging the life of their loved one.

We must realize that a grieving family should not have to bear their pain alone. They need the presence and actions of loving caring people around them to make their days as stress-free as possible. In the Bible, Mary and Martha had friends to be with them after the death of Lazarus. In Job's losses, Job had three friends to sit with him for seven days, showing their support. We should respond to others who have lost a loved one in a way that demonstrates that same kind of support, encouragement, and love.

WORKS CITED

1   Doug Manning, **Don't Take my Grief Away from Me**, (Hereford, Texas: Insight Books, 1979), p. 97.

2   John W. James and Frank Cherry, **The Grief Recovery** Handbook, New York: Harper and Row, 1988), p. 27.

3   Delores Kuenning, **Helping People Through Grief**, (Minneapolis: Bethany House, 1987), p. 258.

4   James and Cherry, 30.

5   Manning, 98.

6   Ibid, 99.

7   James and Cherry, 32.

8   Martha Bittle Clark, **Are You Weeping with me, God?**, (Nashville: Broadman Press, 1987), p. 28.

9   Kuenning, 259.

10   Clark, 50.

11   Mary-jane Creel, **A Little Death**, Killen, Alabama 1987, p. 79.

12   Janice Harris Lord, **No Time for Goodbyes**, (Ventura,

California: Pathfinder Publishing, 1987), p. 105.
13 Clark, 71.
14 James and Cherry, 31.
15 Creel, 82.
16 Ibid, 83.
17 Ibid.
18 Ibid, 84.

Chapter 9

Why Am I Grieving Alone?
How To Cope With Hidden And Unrecognized Sorrows

by Don Williams

At best, caring friends are often at a loss for words when visiting with grieving survivors at the funeral home. Words often escape them when members of the grieving family are seen in the grocery store or some other public place. But what about losses that are not known about or losses that are not typically recognized? What can be said or done then?

Consider the following scenarios. You sit in church by an elderly lady in her eighties. She seems most despondent, and does not talk and chat as she usually does. Her husband died several years ago, and she has lived alone in the old homeplace with a dog that her husband gave her fifteen years ago. The dog recently died and she is depressed but feels people will not understand her feelings. She is embarrassed to tell folks just how sad she really feels.

A father and mother sit in the funeral home, ready to receive visitors due to the loss of their youngest son. He was grown and had left home and moved away. Now he has been brought back to be buried in the family plot at the cemetery. He had lived a short life and died penniless, alone, and with a gun in his hand. He had chosen to end his own life. Now the grieving parents wait but in vain. Some did not know that they had a son.

Others did not know the boy and decide not to go. Still others do not know what to say because of the nature of the death. The end result is that two very lonely and frustrated parents are left to grieve without the benefit of the only support they had; the friends that know and love them. As Kenneth Doka writes, "The paradox of disenfranchised grief is that grief is often intensified while normal supports are lessened."[1]

A young woman is deeply in love with a man whose wife had been killed in a car wreck several years ago. She left behind three very beautiful boys who look at their father's fiancee as a mom. She loves them and spends a great deal of time with them. Suddenly, the father is killed in an unfortunate accident, and the boys are sent to live with other relatives. The young woman feels as if her entire life is nothing but an empty void. Yet others do not understand. After all, she was not related to them. The care and support that she so vitally needs does not come from her best friends.

These and other similar stories are examples of a form of grief that is becoming more and more common in an age of dysfunctional living called *disenfranchised grief*.

> This form of grief is one that people experience when they incur a loss which cannot be openly acknowledged, socially sanctioned, or publicly shared.[2]

Examples of this type of loss has just been given. The older woman was afraid others would not think well of her if she told them about the loss of her dog, so she said nothing. Suicide is one of the "taboo" subjects that no one talks about, so grieving parents had to grieve alone because no one knew what to say or how to respond to their "socially unaccepted loss." Friends might think the young woman silly if she were to tell them how empty she felt over the loss of her fiancee and her "future kids," so she says nothing.

We live in a society that has certain "grieving rules" that are set as a standard for grieving. These rules attempt to specify who, when, where, how, how long, and for whom people should grieve. These rules are often reflected in company personnel policies. In some companies, a person may receive a week off from work in the event of the loss of a spouse or child. They may receive three days off work in the event of the loss of a sibling or parent or grand-parent. Airplane tickets purchased are deemed non-refundable, unless they are turned in due to the loss of a spouse or child. In other words, airplane corporations see only these deaths as deserving of refunding the money. Kenneth Doka in his book on disenfranchised grief writes,

> Such policies reflect the fact that each society defines who has a legitimate right to grieve, and these definitions of right correspond to relationships, primarily familial, that are socially recognized and sanctioned.[3]

It is important to look at what this form of grief involves. This chapter will suggest ways of properly showing care in situations where there is a lack of understanding concerning the loss.

THE RELATIONSHIP IN DISENFRANCHISED GRIEF IS OFTEN NOT RECOGNIZED.

Statements of sorrow are often made based upon the relationship that existed between the deceased and the bereaved. In cases where the relationship is not known or understood, there may be a lack of care and concern demonstrated toward the bereaved.

In the scenario that was mentioned in which the fiancee's boyfriend died, some might wonder why she would be grieving in such a traumatic way. What was not understood was that her future was lost when her boyfriend died. Not only that, the young woman lost the hope of a future family with the moving of the boyfriend's sons to another state. Caring people need to realize the relationship of love and care that is present in any loss. Giving people permission to grieve, even if there was not a biological kinship, can go a long way in alleviating the anger, loneliness, and frustration that can easily be felt in losses where the relationship is not readily recognized.

Other relationships that are not publicly recognized or socially sanctioned can also cause disenfranchised loss. Although condemned by God in His Word, we live in an age where some think nothing of being involved in extramarital affairs and homosexual relationships. Those involved in such relationships are touched by grief when the relationship is terminated by the death of a partner.

Even relationships that existed in the past can still bring forth present and future grief. Ex-spouses, former friends and former business associates can cause family members and friends to feel a great sense of loss when they die. "The death of that significant other can...cause a grief reaction because it brings finality to that earlier loss, ending any remaining contact or fantasy of reconciliation or reinvolvement."[4] Imagine a wife who hears of the death of her ex-husband. He was abusive in his treatment of her, and he was sexually unfaithful to her. Yet, he was the father of their three children and had been good and kind to them. Some would wonder why she would feel any grief at his death; others would be uncertain as to what to say to her because of the nature of the relationship. One can see how relationships of this type might be misunderstood or not accepted. It is important, when a loss occurs, to think through the possible relationships in which this person might have been involved.

THE LOSS IN DISENFRANCHISED GRIEF IS OFTEN NOT RECOGNIZED

In some cases, the loss itself is not socially defined as significant by society. This is often true in perinatal death, the death of a baby through miscarriage or before the child reaches full term.

B. Raphael suggests that Perinatal deaths lead to strong grief reactions, yet research indicates that many significant others still perceive the loss to be relatively minor.[5] Statements like, "Well, it was not meant to be" or "Well, at least you did not get to know it" are often stated to grieving and frustrated parents. Notice that some folks call the baby an "it" instead of a he or she. Sometimes, when a baby is still-born or dies of birth complications, people will say, "I'm sure you will be able to have another, you being so young and all." None of this takes away the fact that this child who was a part of the parents should be alive and is dead, and their hearts are breaking. Loving and caring friends, family and church friends should treat the loss of the baby as if it were the loss of a grown adult or older child. The "wellness" of the baby does not matter in any way. If anything, more attention and care needs to be demonstrated to the grieving survivors because of the nature of the loss.

Although unknown to others, those women who decide to have an abortion go through a great deal of pain as well. Would-be mothers complain of pain in their shoulder and chest areas where the baby would have nursed, or where they might have held and rocked the baby. Those who know of women who abort their babies may not recognize the grief and increased guilt they will go through because of the decision they made.

Another loss that may not be recognized is the loss of a beloved pet. Earlier in this chapter, the scenario was given of the elderly lady grieving and unhappy over the loss of her dog. That dog was given to her by her husband and was the last link of attachment she had with him. The dog would have brought companionship to her and would have given her needed worth and value by giving her something to do. The dog would need to be walked which would give her the opportunity of getting needed exercise as well. Being outside would allow her to visit and talk with significant friends, which would help her in social skills and her own well-being. What some may have seen as "just the death of a dog" was much more than that. Therefore, grief can be complicated when the nature of the loss is not validated. No loss should ever be minimized. "The greatest loss is your loss, whatever it is."

THE GRIEVER IN DISENFRANCHISED GRIEF IS NOT RECOGNIZED

There are situations in which the characteristics of the bereaved are such that others feel that the loss is not accepted or understood.

> Here the person is not socially defined as capable of grief; therefore there is little or no social recognition of his or her sense of loss or need to mourn.[6]

Some have the mistaken notion that children do not have the capacity to grieve; therefore, little if any recognition of their loss is given to them. As will be seen in the next chapter, children do grieve–they just do so differently from adults.

Others may have the misunderstanding that elderly people do not have the capacity to understand that death has taken place. Imagine an elderly aunt in a nursing home who has only nephews and nieces to attend to her needs. If one of those nephews died, she would most likely realize that something had happened. Not including her in at least acknowledging the loss of the nephew could be traumatic.

Mentally challenged persons may also be disenfranchised in grief. Because they are thought to have limited mental and/or physical skills, some may think that a loss of a loved one to a mentally challenged person is insignificant and that their grief emotions will be limited in feeling. Nothing could be further from the truth. Special attention needs to be given to demonstrate to these people that are seen as equally deserving of care, support, and solace.[7]

PROBLEMS CAUSED BY DISENFRANCHISED GRIEF

There are numerous situations in which disenfranchised grief takes place. It can be exhibited even if a death has not been sustained. Imagine a wife who cares daily for her husband who is an invalid because of an accident. Although she deeply loves him, their future has been drastically changed through the accident that "took her husband away." While some might say, "Be glad he is alive," still the loss is real and will be felt. As Doka puts it, "The man she loved is no longer there, and he will never come back. She may be married, but she is really a hidden widow with silent sorrow."[8] This would also apply in a situation where a mate attends to the needs of the other mate who has Alzheimer's.

Another loss often not recognized, but equally stressful, is the loss of a job. When people meet others for the first time, two questions are normally asked: "Do you have kids, and where do you work?" Imagine a couple who have tried to have children and cannot. To make matters worse, the husband was recently released from his job. Or, he interviews for a job but is not chosen. Such loss can be devastating, yet this grief is often not recognized.

Stigmatized deaths such as suicide, AIDS or death due to homicide can also be disenfranchised. In some cases, the grievers may be too embarrassed to admit that loss or to share their grief with others. As Doka writes, "To share that loss with others means that they have to deal with the fears, questions and disapproval of others."[9] Caring people may not know what to say as well, making the grief that much more awkward and embarrassing. The end result is that grieving family members must grieve alone because they are not comforted by significant friends that could be of help but are not.

PROBLEMS THAT DISENFRANCHISED GRIEVERS FACE

Each situation of disenfranchised grief is unique. Individuals will react in their own way. But there are some common problems that all disenfranchised grievers face.

Disenfranchised grievers are often excluded from caring for dying persons. Imagine a mentally challenged son who is not able to be around a mother dying of cancer. Well-meaning folks will think that he is unable to help or perhaps to even grieve, so he is not included in care for the dying mom. In most cases, this is a mistake since caring for the mother allows the child to do "what he can" to express his love for his mother. It also reinforces the reality of her eventual death.

> As painful as it can often be, caring for a dying person can help in the experience of grieving and frequently alleviates guilt, providing

opportunities for closure. It is hard to deny the reality of death when one faces the evidence daily.[10]

Also, disenfranchised grievers are often excluded from funeral rituals. In the scenario just mentioned, the mentally-challenged son may not be taken to the funeral when his mother dies. His grief may become greater because others did not allow him to attend the funeral or say good-bye in his own way.

In other cases, survivors are not invited to attend the funeral (ex-wife, former friends, business associates, etc.).* The relationship they once had with the deceased is unrecognized or ignored, so the pain and guilt becomes more intense. A funeral normally provides family and friends the chance to memorialize and eulogize their beloved. This is made harder when there is no funeral ritual to attend, or former friends and/or relatives are not invited to attend. Imagine an ex-wife who attends the funeral of her ex-husband. With whom does she sit? What will her former family say to her, if anything? How is she to act at his funeral? After all, he was the father of their children and they had a loving relationship for many years. One can see the many problems that disenfranchised grievers can face.

In grief, it is helpful when people recognize the loss of others and are willing to talk with and help them in their journey of grief. As Doka writes,

> Being able to talk about loss and receive help from others can be a healing process. Conversely, not being able to discuss loss, not to feel others' support, complicates grief.[11]

Imagine a young boy who grows up without the benefit of a father to have around. All his male bonding and learning he receives from an aged uncle that lives near him. He grows up, goes to college, and begins work in a big city. Soon after moving there, his beloved uncle dies, and his new company gives him a hard time about taking several days to attend the funeral. To them, the death is nothing more than the death of an elderly uncle. To him, a part of his life has died. Everything he is and everything he hopes to become, he owes to that uncle who was like a dad to him. Also, when he returns back to work, others will not be there to share in his loss, or to talk to him about his emotions because they do not understand the significance of his loss.

In this fast moving, "get-ahead at all costs" kind of world that is called LIFE, disenfranchised losses (deaths that are not readily recognized, publicly shared, or openly acknowledged) will become more common as time goes on. Families are becoming more dysfunctional, and with the breakdown of the home, there seems to be a greater loss of respect for the deceased, as well as their grieving families.

WAYS OF HELPING THOSE EXPERIENCING DISENFRANCHISED GRIEF

Experiences such as divorce and AIDS that can lead to disenfranchised grief shows no signs of abating. As developmentally disabled persons live longer, they too are more likely to experience losses of parents and even siblings.[12]

What can be done to help people through losses that are typically disenfranchised?

First of all, when a friend loses a loved one, reflection ought to be made concerning the relationship they had with that loved one. What did they lose when their loved one died? Was she just an aunt, or was she the mother that the friend never had? Are there other relatives that can provide support and stability to this friend, or was the aunt one of the last relatives she had? Questions such as these can help in understanding the nature of their loss, as well as the feelings that are present because of the loss.

No loss should ever be minimized. Whether it is a friend at work, a pet who has died, or some other loss, it needs to be treated as that, A LOSS! The greatest loss is whatever one has, whatever it is. When people feel comfortable to let others in on their grief, part of the isolation of disenfranchised grief will be gone.

Another thing that can be done is to find ways to acknowledge the loss.[13] Letters, poems, or memorials written or given in memory of a loved one goes a long way in letting the family know that their loss was recognized, and that their loved one was loved by others. A mother lost her teen age daughter when she decided to take her own life. On the day when the daughter would have turned eighteen, the grieving mother received word that good friends had planted a tree in the park where the young girl had played, as a memorial of her life. Actions like this can be of great comfort and help.[14]

Finally, respect must be given to the emotions and feelings of all people, young and old, developmentally disabled, the confused, distressed, and disoriented. As Doka writes, they "may not always understand or express loss in traditional ways, but that does not mean their attachments are not felt nor that their losses are not grieved."[15]

Grief is one of the deepest emotions that anyone will feel. Regardless of the age or intellectual mentality of any person, people will grieve in their own way. Society can do no greater thing than to allow them to grieve in the way they can, and support and encourage them in their grief. Doug Manning writes that the worst discomfort in the world is "watching a friend hurt and having no answer."[16] Worse than even this, in this writer's opinion, is *watching a friend hurt all alone.*

WORKS CITED

1   Kenneth J. Doka, **Handout on Disenfranchised Grief**, Conference on Disenfranchised Grief, Tuscaloosa, Alabama, February 3, 1994.

2   Ibid.

3   Kenneth J. Doka, **Disenfranchised Grief**, (Lexington, Massachusetts: Lexington Books, 1989), p. 4.

4   Ibid, 5.

5   B. Raphael, **The Anatomy of Bereavement**, New York: Basic Books.

6   Doka,   Disenfranchised, 6.

7   Ibid, 6,7.

8   Kenneth J.Doka, "Grief: Coping with Hidden Sorrow", **Bereavement** (May, 1992), p. 6.

9   Ibid.

10   Ibid.

11   Ibid.

12   Ibid,7.

13   Ibid.

14   Video, Howard Clinebell, **Healing Your Grief Wound: The Latter Stages.**

15   Doka, Bereavement, 7.

16   Doug Manning, **Don't Take my Grief Away from Me,** (Hereford, Texas: Insight Books, 1979), p. 94.

Chapter 10

What Do I Tell The Children?

The Subject Of Grief And Children

by Don Williams

It was the first time she had seen "Daddy Jack" for a matter of days. His cancer had caused continued deterioration, until he was in a coma-like state. Finally, death came mercifully, and my friend was gone. He was many things in this life-a lawyer, an airplane pilot instructor, a construction builder, a political campaign manager, a Bible school teacher, but most of all, a christian and a friend.

Now as I stood at his coffin, the family came to see him in his rested state. As the little five-year-old great grand-child saw him and touched his hand, she said, "why is Daddy Jack so cold?" She also wanted to know what would happen if you were to raise his eyelid.

Her child-like questions caused me to think back almost twenty-five years earlier, when I was facing the loss of my beloved granddad, J.E.Williams. How I had loved him! He was the first gospel preacher in the family, as well as an educator and a poet. I loved to walk with him, almost having to run to stay up with his long strides. In the summer before he died, it was announced he had "cancer." I did not really know what it was, and so was not ready for the demise of his physical condition. When I saw him later, I was almost scared of him. What had happened to the robust "granddiddy" (as I called him) that I knew?

Christmas came, and he was weaker and sicker. He died the last of January, and when we came for his funeral, I did not know what to expect. As a preacher's kid, I had been to funerals, but not to a close relative's funeral. This was different than the other funerals I had attended. This was a funeral for someone I loved dearly.

As I approached the casket and looked at him, a older female cousin told me," Think of this as only his remains. What we knew and loved him for is not there—that part is within us and will always be there. This is just what is left behind." This made me feel better, and I could look at him (and even touch him) without it really bothering me.

DEATH AND CHILDREN

In early America, death was a familiar experience. When several generations of a family lived in the same house, children became aware of aging, illness and death. With life somewhat like that of **"The Waltons,"** children watched as Grandpa and Grandma grew old and eventually died. They gathered with other family members when death occurred, and knew what funerals and "wakes" were all about. These were normally held in the home.

Children of early America realized that a significant loss had occurred, and they would experience tears and sorrow. Death was something that was a regular part of their lives as animals would regularly die. Death was not a mystery to children in early America.

Today, children live in a "grief-avoiding" culture.[1] For many reasons, children in the United States often grow up without being exposed to the pain of grief during childhood. Many live in an urban environment. Also, modern medicine and technological advances have drastically reduced infant and child mortality, while at the same time prolonging the life of the aged. In addition to this, more and more aged people live their latter years separated from family in places like nursing homes, retirement care facilities, etc. Thus, families and especially children do not witness the decline and eventual death of aunts and uncles or even grandparents. "Consequently, many children do not have the opportunity to experience the normal grief that accompanies these events."[2]

•When a death occurs for a family member, the homeplace becomes a whirlwind of activity. The phone begins to ring constantly, neighbors come and go, and other relatives may pop in unexpectedly. Often, the children, referred to as the "forgotten mourners,"[3] cannot make sense of what is going on. Worse, they are unintentionally neglected as major decisions concerning the funeral are made. Doug Manning suggests that this can bring on feelings of insecurity and rejection. Chaos can become the "order of the day" around the house, as people come and go, get ready for the funeral, etc. As children are lost in the shuffle, they may feel that they are unimportant, or they would have been remembered.[4] Manning reminds us that "children feel, even if they do not understand. Understanding comes later–the feelings need a hug."[5]

It is important, when death occurs, for a safe, predictable system of child care to be set up.

> If a child knows he can trust someone to feed, clothe, bathe, and love him, he can then participate in the grieving of the family. Otherwise, fears for his physical survival, withdrawal, and anger will be primary.[6]

WHAT TO DO WHEN DEATH OCCURS

When a death of a loved one occurs, a parent or someone close to the child should tell them that the death has taken place. News of one's death travels quickly, and one needs to tell the children the "truth of the matter" before they hear it from others. Often information about a death is distorted when told by others.

Some think that it is best to shield children from death by not telling them that their loved one has died, or by sending them away for the days prior to and of the funeral.[7] Not allowing children to deal with death, or even excluding them from the events of the death, will only harm the child.

> Your child has a right and a need to be included. She must be allowed to share in the grief with those she loves. Silence about the death and isolation from important others at this time deprive her of the opportunity to deal with her own emotions...Additionally, the fantasies of children are often much worse than reality. If you do not explain what is going on, children will start to draw their own conclusions, which may cause problems later on.[8]

Once they have been told that a loved one has died, parents or other relatives need to tell them what will happen next. They need to be told about the visitation, or "wake," if there is one, and about the funeral that will follow. No doubt, there will be many questions, and the number of questions will depend upon the age and previous experience the child has had with loss.[9]

TO ATTEND OR NOT TO ATTEND
THE FUNERAL

Often, when a death occurs, some parents decide that it would be best for their children not to attend a funeral. The writer conducted a funeral for a man whose grandchildren were coming to the funeral home for the very first time. The children were teens and had never been to a funeral. They were afraid of coming, but after being there for the visitation, they decided to stay and attend the funeral as well.

The decision for kids to attend the funeral should be based on their age and other factors. Babies and children under two may be able to determine that parents (especially the mother) may be upset, but they are not able to ascertain that a death has occurred. Kids that are older should be encouraged to attend the funeral, but they should not be forced into going. Yet, as previously stated, to shield kids from death is a terrible mistake. To shut a youngster out of the funeral experience might be quite costly and damaging to his future development. He is an integral part of the family unit and should participate with them on this sad but momentous occasion. However, if the child is unwilling, he should not be forced to go or made to feel guilty because "he let the family down." If he does not attend the funeral, it may be wise to provide an opportunity at some later time to visit the cemetery and see the grave.[10]

The reason for having a funeral ought to be given to the child. Funerals provide a unique opportunity for the natural expression of grief and allow those attending to express thanks for the privilege of knowing and loving the person who died. Funerals provide the chance to remember the life of the one who died, offer words of comfort to the remaining survivors, and re-affirm the fact that life continues on until the day that death comes to us.

Parents would do well to keep in mind the following suggestions regarding children and funerals: take your children to a funeral of someone to whom they were not significantly close. This will provide an opportunity for them to watch what goes on without being emotionally involved. Children need to be told what will be going on during the funeral (flowers, prayer, scripture reading, lesson, how long the funeral will last, etc.).

Children need to know that the people they see at the funeral will probably be expressing a wide range of emotions. Some may cry or sob, while others may laugh. They need to know it is natural to cry.[11] This suggestion cannot be over-emphasized. Grief is hard enough for adults to deal with, much less children. To add to their sadness the edict that as a boy or a girl, they "are to hold it in and be a man" or "be a woman" is not only wrong, it is merciless.

> Tears are the first and most natural tribute that can be paid to the one who is gone. The child misses the deceased. He wishes the loved one were still with him. The son and daughter whose father dies should express their grief. It is natural. They loved him. They missed him...Tears are the tender tribute of yearning affection for those who have died but can never be forgotten. The worst thing possible is for the child to repress them. The child who stoically keeps his grief bottled up inside may later find a release in a more serious explosion to his inner makeup.[12]

At the same time, children should not feel guilty if they do not express grief through crying or tears. Mary-Jane Creel, who lost a baby that lived less than two months, wrote,

> If children do not ask questions, it does not mean their minds are not working and thinking about the death that has occurred. It probably means they are too afraid of finding out

something bad, of upsetting their parents, or that they do not know what to ask to help themselves...Do not expect them to grieve as long and as intensely as you. At first, the death will have a pronounced position in your family's everyday lives. This should pass with time, and everyone will gain more perspective as the weeks go by...Your children should not be forced to grieve or made to feel guilty because they are happy again.[13]

One needs to remember that a child's relationship with the deceased has not ended but changed. After the funeral, it is wise to keep pictures and other reminders of the deceased around to spark conversation with your child about their loss. Do not be afraid to mention the deceased by name, and allow your children to talk about the deceased as they desire. All this can help form a new set of emotional bonds with the person who died.[14]

VARIOUS WAYS CHILDREN EXPRESS THEMSELVES IN GRIEF

When children lose a loved one in death, they will express their feelings in a variety of ways. The ways they express themselves will depend upon their age, their mental and physical development, and their relationship with the deceased.[15] Although more is known about a child's reactions to the loss of a parent than that of a brother or sister,[16] some of the dimensions of grief will be the same.

The following is a list of twelve dimensions of grief commonly experienced by bereaved children. The list is not all inclusive nor mutually exclusive. These grief responses occur in no specific order or progression. As is the case with adults in grief, there is no script or certain order for the dimensions of grief in children. Each child's responses are uniquely different. The dimensions are as follows: Apparent lack of feelings, Physiological changes, Regression behavior, "Big Man" or "Big Woman" Syndrome, Disorganization and Panic, Explosive Emotions, Acting-out Behavior, Fear, Guilt and Self Blame, Relief, Loss and Loneliness, and Reconciliation. Some of these dimensions will now be discussed.

Apparent lack of Feelings. Children often respond to the death of a loved one with emotional shock and an apparent lack of feelings. They can be playing in the yard only minutes after learning of the death of a loved one. Although adults might think this strange, this behavior is a protective mechanism and nature's way of caring for children. It allows them to detach themselves from the pain in the only way they can.[17] Children do not have the mental ability of grieving for an extended period of time. Thus, when children resume playing or act as if they did not hear the terrible news of a loved one's death, they are only doing what they can do to deal with their pain.

This writer has seen this happen several times at funerals. At the funeral home or funeral, a child may be crying and grieving the loss of their loved one. Fifteen minutes later, at the cemetery, they may be playing "kick the rock" with cousins or friends. The loss and pain has been too great, and they are escaping it for a period of time.

Also, we as adults would do well not to misinterpret the idea of playing. Unless a child is extremely young, he or she has the ability to understand that a death has taken place. Their play may be a form of their working through the problems of their loss.

> Play is the natural means of communication for a child, offering safe avenues for self-expression. It enables her to experiment with

different identities and to rehearse difficult or anxiety-provoking events...Oftentimes when children play death games or act out funerals, it is because they are trying to master their loss, as well as take a break from their grief.[18]

Regression Behavior. Under the normal stress of grief, children often return to a sense of protection and security they experienced at an earlier time in their lives. This need may be demonstrated in a number of ways: the desire to be held or rocked, even though they have "outgrown" this need; not wanting to get too far away from·parents; or even requests for parents to do simple tasks they normally do, like tying shoes, or helping them get dressed. They may have difficulty in working alone at school. Some smaller children may go back to a form of talking "baby talk," become afraid of the dark, or other such actions.[19]

This can happen if a boy loses a mother. He may begin to suck his thumb and whine a great deal. He may begin to demand a great deal of attention from adults. He is saying in effect: "Dear Mother, see, I am only a very little baby. Please love me and stay with me."[20]

Regressive behavior normally occurs immediately following a death. If children are allowed the freedom of returning to a younger, safer time for awhile, they will usually emerge from their mourning more competent. Such regressive behavior is usually temporary. As long as children know that someone will care and love and support them, then they feel safe and they will be able to deal with their grief.[21]

"Big-Man" or "Big-Woman" Syndrome. The opposite of regression behavior is demonstrated where the child attempts to grow up quickly and exhibit adult behavior in an attempt to replace the person who has died. This forced maturity can be the result of simply carrying out the instructions of respected adults who say "You'll now have to be the man (or woman) of the house."[22]

Although they mean well, such adults are unaware of the potentially damaging impact of this message. "Sometimes a child unconsciously adopts this syndrome as a symbolic means of trying to keep the one who had died alive. By filling this loved one's role, a child doesn't have to acknowledge the full effect of the loss on his or her life."[23] Children are just that, children, and try as they might, they are not able to be an adult for any sensible amount of time. Adults must not become dependent on their child for their own nurture. "While your grieving can be shared and can bring you closer to each other, the child will sense your neediness if you become to dependent on him, It is too big a load for him to carry."[24]

Adults can take a major step in preventing "forced" maturity by not allowing adults to hand out advice such as "You'll have to take care of your mom now that your dad is gone" or "You are now the head of the house and will have to make the major decisions." Such comments only result in the development of frustrated or depressed children who are not allowed to grieve in ways conducive to their ages.[25]

Explosive Emotions. This dimension of grief is often the most upsetting for adults. It is hard to know how to respond to children who explode with such emotions as anger, blame, hatred, resentment, rage and jealousy. Behind these emotions are a child's primary feeling of pain, frustration, helplessness, fear and hurt caused by the death of a loved one. "Anger and other related emotions are natural, intelligent responses by a child in an effort to restore the valued relationship that has been lost."[26] Like an adult, anger can be directed at any number of people-a parent or sibling, a teacher, friends, the hospital, or even God. The fact that the dead person does not come back to life, despite the explosive emotions, is part of the reality testing that children need in order to get through their grief and heal properly. Although confusing to adults, children need this form of expressing their emotions in order to protest and deal with the loss that is real. "Children who either do not give themselves permission to protest, or don't receive permission from others, may turn their anger inward. The result is low self-esteem, depression, chronic feelings of guilt and physical complaints."[27]

Parents can be of great help in this time of great emotion by allowing children to express their emotions. As long as they do not hurt themselves or others, parents need to understand that the "safe world" of their child has been violated, and they are dealing with this loss in the only way they know how to.[28] Sometimes being mean to their best friend, or kicking their dog, is a form of expressing their grief. It is not being suggested that such anger gives children the license to hurt others. It is being suggested that these are ways that children often act out their feelings. Parents need to give them a safe environment to express their feelings, while at the same time encouraging them to do so in a non-violent manner.

Guilt and Self-Blame. Children, more than adults, are more likely to feel guilt over the loss of a loved one. In their "little" minds they decide that since bad things happen when you are "naughty," they must have done something to have caused the death of their loved one. The death of a parent must be retribution for their wrongdoing. Children then search their minds for the "bad deed" that caused their parent's death.

Young children take words and ideas too literal. They can believe that if something is said, then it must come to pass. Therefore, if in anger they once said, "I hate you and hope you die, Mom" and then the mother does die in an accident or something, they feel responsible and feel guilty for causing the mother's death by what they said.

What can be done about helping children work through their guilt? First of all, it is important to allow the child to express their anxieties.

> In his childish mind he may remember times when he may not have been so good to this person as he should have been. Let him know that all people try to be good and loving but do not always succeed. Nor does one have to.[29]

Secondly, parents should explain that all people die. They should avoid linking suffering and death with sin and punishment. They might point out the death of a loved neighbor and show that they were good and kind, yet they still died. No one did "anything" to cause their death; it just happened. If the cause of death is known, a caring adult needs to explain in simple terms why the person died. The child needs to understand that what they did or said did not cause the death of the parent or someone else, and that it will not cause their death.[30]

Finally, explain to children that "wishing does not make it so." Show them that just by saying words, or even by thinking words does not automatically cause something to happen.

> Try to recall those happy moments when the child did make the deceased very happy. For the youngster who is too young to give shape to his thoughts or to find the words which might relieve his guilt, the best therapy is through relationships with other people. Children learn self-acceptance by being accepted by others.[31]

Reconciliation: The final dimension. Reconciliation is the final dimension of healthy grief for children. Like adults, they never get over grief, but can become reconciled and can adapt to it. They finally come to the realization that life will be different without the presence of the person they loved who is now dead. They can now accept this, and feel a renewed sense of energy and confidence in life again, which results in getting involved in various activities once again.

As with adults, there is no specific timetable for children to reach the point of reconciliation. A child will proceed at their own pace, depending on age, personality, social environment and relationship to the person who has ᐧdied. Changes that suggest a child is reaching reconciliation include these things: a return to normal eating and sleepɪng patterns, a renewed sense of well-being, an increase in thinking and judgment capabilities, an increased ability to enjoy life's experiences, a recognition of the finality of the death, and the establishment of new and healthy relationships.

> Pcrhaps the most important gain in the reconciliation process is the child's ability to successfully cope with the loss. The child has come to terms with grief and is ready to get on with the business of living.[32]

THE AGE OF CHILDREN AND DEATH

Much has been written about the way death affects the lives of children, based upon their mental and physical development. Space will not permit an exhaustive discussion of this subject, but suffice it to say, children are affected by death. To what extent they are affected depends upon their age, their sensitivity, and their relationship to the person who died.

Children under two will have no understanding of death, but will have a general feeling of something being wrong. They will realize that "things" are not as they usually are, and that dad and mom are upset over something. Special care and attention needs to be given in terms of holding and touching children of this age during this time. If children are sent away, parents need to make sure that they are well taken care of.

Children ages three to five will have some awareness that something bad has happened. They will not understand death to any degree of depth. They may feel insecure; thus holding and touching becomes very important. They will have questions about death and about what has happened. The answers parents give need to be as simple as their questions. Do not tell them anymore than what they ask. At the same time, do not brush them off by saying "You are too young to understand." That will do nothing but add to their insecurity.

Children ages six to eight will likely have more questions about death. Answer their questions calmly and honestly. Do not give them an opportunity to draw their own conclusions as to what happened. Often these conclusions are wrong and can cloud their thinking for years to come. I can remember some children of this age that I was talking to after the death of their great-grandfather. I was taking the three of them to play with my children, while the family made the necessary arrangements. One of them made the statement, "Well, Papa is dead, and he was old, so I guess MaMa will be next. Then, there is uncle Vercie-he is sick and old, so I guess he will die soon too." Bless his heart, the child was hurting over the loss of his beloved great-grandfather, and had it figured out that all his other older relatives would have to die, and die soon. It was explained to him that it did not happen that way, and this hopefully helped him in his thinking.

Children ages nine to twelve will understand death

to a surprising degree. They will relate the events of the death in their own terms. They may talk about the race car that they were working on, and now because of the death, cannot finish. They may talk about the trip that was going to be taken, or the fishing they were going to do, but now this is not possible. This may sound selfish, but it allows them to express the way they feel in the world they are living in at that time. Children of this age should be allowed to talk, and should be included in the funeral process. They need care, support and love during the time of their grieving.

•Adolescents ages thirteen to sixteen are at a difficult age. Feelings, thoughts, emotions, and physical growth are trying to develop at the same time. When death interferes with what is already a complicated mix, then it can cause feelings of guilt, depression, an increased awareness of their own mortality, and confusion.[33]

Added to this is the fact that many of the deaths that teens observe are unexpected and traumatic. A parent or grandparent dies of a heart attack, or a peer of their acquaintance is killed in a car wreck. This threatens their own existence, as well as causing feelings about how unfair death is. As teens grow and begin to become independent, their grief work in time of death becomes complicated. They find it difficult to accept the intensity of the painful feelings of grief they are experiencing, yet they do not want to receive help from adults in coping with such feelings.

Often, unrealistic social expectations are placed on bereaved teens. Since they are in the process of reaching manhood or womanhood, some adults may suggest to them that they need to be grown-up and mature as they face death. This is especially true, if there are younger siblings still left to raise in the family. When this occurs, teenagers do not give themselves, nor are they given, permission to mourn.

Most peers do not have a proper grasp of death, and thus do not know what to do or say when their friends lose a loved one. Whereas adults have a group of mutual caregivers (adults) to grieve with them, the very people who mean a great deal to teens (their peers) are either indifferent, or at best, unable to provide them with the social and emotional support they need in the loss of a loved one.[34]

Grief is greatly complicated by the many pressures that an adolescent must face. Parents and loving caregivers will do well to show extra care and compassion to teens who are grieving over the loss of a friend or relative. Special attention needs to be given to avoid offering advice, or to suggest that they act like mature adults when that is not possible.

In a sense, these words would apply to children of any age. Grief is difficult for adults. It is unfair, but one has to realize that their children will also grieve when they lose a loved one. It is hard to help your kids when parents are hurting themselves. If one can remember to answer the questions children ask, deal with the children where they are, include them in the funeral process as much as possible, and allow them to grieve in their own way, then one will go a long way in helping their children through their grief journey, as well as helping themselves in the process.

WORKS CITED

1   Alan D. Wolfelt, **A Child's View of Death,** (Fort Collins, Colorado: Center for Loss and Life Transition, 1991), p. 8.

2   Ibid, 9.

3   Ibid, 6.

4   Doug Manning, **Don't Take my Grief Away from**

Me, (Hereford, Texas: Insight Books, 1979), p. 26.

5   Ibid, 22.

6   Janice Harris Lord, **No Time for Goodbyes**, (Ventura, California: Pathfinder Publishing, 1987), p. 80.

7   Brochure, "Children and Death", National Funeral Directors Association, Inc., (Milwaukee, Wisconsin) p. 1.

8   Therese A. Rando, **How to go on Living when Someone You Love Dies**, (New York: Bantam Books, 1988), p. 202.

9   Brochure, 1.

10   Earl A. Grollman, Editor, **Explaining Death to Children,** (Boston: Beacon Press, 1967), p. 24.

11   Wolfelt, 28,29.

12   Grollman, 17,18.

13   Mary-jane Creel, **A Little Death**, Killen, Alabama, 1987, pp. 12,14.

14   Brochure, 4.

15   Wolfelt, 14.

16   Rando, 199.

17   Wolfelt, 14.

18   Rando, 201.

19   Wolfelt, 15.

20   Grollman, 16.

21   Wolfelt, 15.

22   Ibid, 16.

23   Ibid.

24   Lord, 81.

25   Wolfelt, 17.

26   Ibid, 17,18.

27   Ibid, 18.

28   Ibid.

29   Grollman, 22,23.

30   Lord, 80.

31   Grollman, 23.

32   Wolfelt, 22,23.

33   Manning, 23-25.

34   Wolfelt, 35-38.

Chapter 11

Preacher, Can You Take Away My Grief?

The Dilemma That Ministers And Other Caregivers Face In Grief Support

by Ron Williams

There was once a minister who lived a long time ago that was a very close friend with a particular family. Of all the people that this minister knew and loved, this family which consisted of a brother and two sisters, seemed to be especially close to him. You might have heard of this minister; his name was Jesus! His close friends were Lazarus, and Lazarus's two sisters, Martha and Mary.

In John chapter eleven, John records how Jesus dealt with this family in regard to their experience of grief. John tells us that Lazarus died and had been buried for four days when Christ came and visited Martha and Mary in their city of Bethany. Notice John chapter eleven, verse thirty through verse thirty six:

> Now Jesus had not yet come into the town, but was in the place where Martha met Him. Then the Jews who were with her in the house, and comforting her, when they saw Mary rose up quickly and went out, followed her, saying, 'She is going to the tomb to weep there.' Then, when Mary came where Jesus was, and saw Him, she fell down at His feet, saying to Him, 'Lord, if You had been here, my brother would not

have died.' Therefore, when Jesus saw her weeping, and the Jews who came with her weeping, He groaned in the spirit and was troubled. And He said, 'Where have you laid him?' They said to Him, 'Lord, come and see.' Jesus wept. Then the Jews said, 'See how He loved him!'

Death! It is inevitable! It is inescapable! We can spend money on physical fitness, we can go to the best doctors, we can try to eat the right kinds of food, but eventually, or suddenly, death becomes a reality for all of us!

The vocation of a minister is unique in that he deals with life from two very distinct and different vantage points. Ministers welcome the births of children into families of congregations that they work with, yet at the same time they deal with the deaths of church members as well. It is here that ministers come to understand the principle that the Apostle Paul gave when he said to "Rejoice with those that rejoice and to weep with those that weep," Romans 12: 15. Typically, in most cases, it is far easier to rejoice with families over the birth of their children than it is to weep with those that weep over the death of their loved ones.

Ministers and other caregivers need to recognize that there is not a more human emotion or feeling more powerful than the emotion of grief. Of all of the things that we experience in this life, grief is that one UNIVERSAL emotion that will be felt by every human being. Grief is not something that people can choose to avoid, shun, or escape. Ministers should remember that grief will be a part of their own personal lives and their church members as well.

Ministers need to understand that when a church member loses a loved one in death, the minister can play an important part in comforting the grieving family. Ministers should realize the very important role that they will play in the lives of that grieving family from the outset of their grief experience. Martha Bittle Clark, in her book, **Are You Weeping With Me, God?**, illustrates the minister's role so candidly when she was informed of her daughter's tragic death from a car accident. Looking for her minister Herman R. Yoos, she wrote,

> Where are you, Herman? I keep dialing and dialing you at church and there is no answer. I even tried calling you at home. I need you. No one else can help. You must make God understand how much I love Sherry—and how I can't let her go! At least, not yet. Not at eighteen. Not from a wreck that wasn't even her fault.[1]

In her book which was a culmination of journal entries that she made as she was grieving, she wrote the following entry the day after she had searched for her minister in vain. She wrote:

> Herman has stayed with us most of the day, and I am glad. He is my only connection to Sherry and to heaven. He prayed with us and asked you to comfort us in our sorrow. I don't think he knows that my heart is too full of anger to pray to you, myself.[2]

It is rather difficult for the minister to realize what their role will be in dealing with the grieving family. Because each grief situation is different, the minister needs to allow for that difference in dealing with families within their congregation or community. Let the minister never forget that GRIEF IS INDIVIDUALISTIC and every family will deal with their sorrow and grief in their own unique way.

Because of the minister's association to the grieving family as their minister, the family may begin to expect at least two things from the minister as their caregiver. Number one, they may expect the minister to answer all of their questions about the grief incident. "Preacher, why did this happen?" They might say, "How could God do this to us?" "Why did this happen to us now?" "Where was God when we needed Him the most?" They might even ask, "Why would a God of love do this to people that love Him?" Grieving families that are hurting from the pain of grief will expect their minister and other caregivers to answer their questions concerning grief.

Number two, they would like for their minister to try and make everything all right again. Because of the excruciating pain that they might be experiencing (perhaps for the very first time), they want the minister to try and undo the damage that has been done. They want the minister to make everything right again for them.

Herein lies the problem that ministers and other caregivers begin to experience as they begin working with families that have been forced to deal with some great trauma in their lives. First of all, a minister cannot answer all of their questions! Regardless of how perceptive and intelligent the caregiver might be, there are some tragedies of life and death that have no real answer. Secondly, a minister cannot make everything all right again for the grieving family. Unlike Jesus with Martha and Mary in John chapter eleven, the minister does not have the ability to bring "their Lazarus" back to life again. Pain, gloom, and despair will become a part of their lives for a period of time and there is no simple phrase or word remedy that will erase that period of bereavement that must take place.

MINISTERS AND THE FAITH PROBLEM

As ministers, we understand the tremendous importance that biblical faith plays in our every day walk of life. We realize the value of such scriptures as 1 Corinthians 15:17, "And if Christ is not risen, your faith is futile; you are still in your sins." We appreciate what the Apostle Paul wrote in 2 Corinthians 5: 7, "For we walk by faith, not by sight." The Hebrew writer wrote continuously on the importance of faith in a person's life. In Hebrews 11: 1, the author said, "Now faith is the substance of things hoped for, the evidence of things not seen." Ministers certainly believe in the power and the presence of faith in a person's every day decisions of life.

It needs to be realized, however, that grieving people may perceive that ministers have what these people would call "a God problem." Because ministers have a faith and a conviction in God that is so strong (and rightly so), these grieving people may feel that their minister does not understand that one's conviction is not enough when they are doubting God because of what has happened to them. When a family is in the throes of depression or anger due to the death of a loved one, their faith in God will be tested like never before. Ministers need to be aware of this great possibility and need to be especially careful not to be appalled at the doubts and feelings that these grieving members may be experiencing. Unless that minister becomes that bridge from God to that despairing family, unless that caregiver helps the grieving family see God through their grief, a gap may form that may take years for that family to work through.

It is also the case that if a minister has not dealt with some kind of grief loss within his own life, that minister may not be able to "weep with those that weep" (Romans 12:15). If that minister has not "walked through the valley of the shadow of death" (Psalm 23:4), as those church members have been forced to do, the minister may not appear to be a person of comfort to someone having to deal with their agony of grief.[3]

A CLASSIC EXAMPLE OF HOW A MINISTER OUGHT TO DEAL WITH GRIEF

John chapter eleven is a wonderful example of noticing how our Lord dealt with the grief of Martha and Mary over the death of their brother, Lazarus. Notice from the text some four points of how Jesus dealt with these grieving people and how ministers today can deal with their church members that grieve.

Point number one, be real. Notice John 11:35, "Jesus wept." That is a very powerful expression, isn't it? Besides memorizing that verse as a child for memory work in Bible class, have you ever thought as to what that verse suggests about Jesus? Jesus wept, He cried, John 11:34 says that "He groaned in the spirit," and that is a very expressive phrase in the original language. Jesus felt the need to be human in his emotions over the death of his friend, Lazarus. When a minister is moved with emotion over the death of a church member, he should not feel ashamed to cry. If the minister is overwhelmed with sorrow and compassion, admit it. While ministers certainly are people that believe firmly in the hope of a better life in the hereafter, they are humans as well. If grieving people see ministers as real and genuine people, then they will feel far more comfortable to grieve within their presence. Be real!

Point number two, be quiet. In John 11, verses 21 and 32, Martha and Mary seem to rebuke the Lord for not being present to prevent their brother from dying. In the verses following these rebukes, one does not find Jesus stating some theological answer to their statements. Jesus was quiet. In a time of trauma and great sorrow, a minister's presence, and not his words, will be most appreciated! Jesus knew that in grief, there is a time to talk and there is a time to listen. Be quiet!

Point number three, be supportive. In John 11, verses 31 and 34, one finds Jesus and "the Jews" coming to show their love and support for the two sisters. Ministers who comfort their church members must have a tender heart of understanding. They should come to be with the family during their time of sorrow NOT OUT OF DUTY but out of love and genuine concern. One of the most effective ways to heal a grieving heart is to have someone support and love you. Be supportive!

Point number four, be available. In John 12:1-2, the text indicates that Jesus had visited Bethany again and had spent time with the family. I believe that it is interesting to notice that even after the miraculous raising of Lazarus, Christ had come back to be with the family. Jesus wanted them to know that He was there for them. Jesus knew that this family had been through a great trauma in their lives, and even though Lazarus had been raised by the power of God, Jesus wanted them to know that He was there for them. So many people make the mistake of forgetting the bereaved family a few days after the funeral service. They quit visiting, calling, or sending cards to them. Unfortunately, this is exactly the time when the shock begins to wear off and the real pain of grief begins to take effect. This is exactly the time when a real caregiver can be of great service to the family. This is exactly the time when a minister needs to communicate to that family, "I am here for you and I am available to your needs." It should always be the case that a few days after the funeral that the minister expresses genuine concern to the church member by asking them, "How are you feeling?" "What can I do to help you in your grief?" Be available![4]

SOME THINGS THAT A MINISTER CAN DO FOR PEOPLE IN GRIEF

The following suggestions are practical things that ministers and other caregivers can say or do for people that are grieving. It should be remembered that grieving people can tell the difference between one who truly cares and others that do something out of duty for them in their grief. Genuine caregivers will remember that as they strive to "weep with those that weep."

Number one: Acknowledge the loss with a call, card, letter, and/or visit.

Number two: Simply say, "I am so sorry," "Words fail me," "I share in your grief," or "I love you."

Number three: Remember that a sympathizing tear, a warm embrace, an arm around the shoulder, or a squeeze of the hand convey your sympathy.

Number four: Give the bereaved family permission to grieve in your presence.

Number five: Listen nonjudgmentally to the grieving family's thoughts and feelings.

Number six: Allow the family to talk about their deceased loved one. Allow them to mention their name in conversations with you.

Number seven: Tell the family that you and others will be praying for them on a continual basis during their period of bereavement.

Number eight: Share a pleasant memory or story of the deceased with the grieving family. Let them know how special their loved one was to you and others.

Number nine: Remember the family on the first anniversaries, birthdate, wedding date, and the death date.

Number ten: Arrange caregivers to help with the readjustment back to church, school, work, etc. Be there for them as they make adjustments in their life.

Number eleven: Visit the grieving family with a core team of compassionate caregivers frequently during the first year of their grief. Arrange for caregivers to take food by or help the family out in some positive manner.

Number twelve: Remember that nothing you can say or do will stop the grieving family's pain instantly. The grieving experience is just not that easy!

Conclusion

Grieving people need ministers to model the example of Jesus in dealing with them and their shattered lives. They need ministers to be real and genuine people around them. They need ministers to listen to them and hear them through their pain. They need ministers to support them and help them as they work through their grief. They need ministers to be available and not forget them as they begin the task of real grieving after the funeral is over. In other words, they need ministers to allow them to grieve as Jesus allowed Martha and Mary to grieve. Jesus believed, as ministers should, that people are healed of grief only when they are allowed to express it to the fullest. We have many in our world today that are grieving, but where in this world are the comforters?

WORKS CITED

1   Clark, Martha Bittle. **Are You Weeping with Me, God?** Nashville: Broadman Press, 1987, p. 12.

2   Clark, p. 13.

3   Thanks and appreciation must go to Bill McDonald of Centerville, Tennessee for the thoughts of the outline used in the introduction of this chapter.

4   Swindoll, Charles R. **Killing Giants, Pulling Thorns**. Portland, OR: Multnomah Press, 1982, pp. 39-40.

Chapter 12

Can I Make It Until January Second?

A Discussion Of Grief And The Holidays

by Don Williams

Her name was Nancy, and she had lost a daughter in a car wreck back in the summer (names have been changed to respect their identity). Ann, her daughter, would have been a senior. She was selling advertisement for the school yearbook when her car was struck by another car and she was killed.

Nancy came to the grief support class I taught, along with two other relatives. In the class, we take a break in the class routine the week of Thanksgiving, and then normally meet two more times before Christmas. The week after Thanksgiving, we met and I asked the class how the holiday had gone and if everyone had "made it as well as possible." Nancy then told the following story:

"It was the first holiday I was going to have to face without my beloved Ann. I went to my mother's house, hoping that there we could reminisce, talking of what made Ann so very special. Instead, no one mentioned her name; it was as if they were afraid to do so. Finally, a cousin said her name without thinking, and then gasped as if it was wrong to bring up the subject. An uneasy silence came over the room, and then my own mother said, 'Nancy, it has been three months-you need to get on with your life!' The very idea-the people who I thought would have loved me, supported me, and helped me in the worst of times were instead afraid to talk about my loss. My husband and I left right then and there and I told him, if that is the care and support and way I am going to be treated, I do not even want to go back at Christmas."

Sadly, this story could be told countless times by many other grieving people—only the names would be changed. The word HOLIDAY normally conjures up thoughts of joy and laughter, families being together eating, the giving of gifts, sharing time and love with each other. It is a time of remembrance of past celebrations, present get-togethers, and a hope for the future.

Yet for about two million families in America each year, it is a time where they "lethargically stumble through the holidays" because they have lost a loved one this year. Thousands of other families who have lost someone in years past hope that this Christmas will be better than previous ones.[1] As Therese Rando says, "as much as you'd like to skip from November to January 2nd, this is impossible."[2]

For grieving families who are in their journey in the valley of grief (some for the first time), HOLIDAYS are nothing more than a painful reminder of the way things used to be. It is a time of mixed emotions, of being overwhelmed with multiple demands, and the real pain of loves lost.

This is not helped by the American family ideal of Christmas. Mass media would have us believe that everything is bright and wonderful in everyone's life. Commercials depict happy kids getting all the toys they want. Television shows and movies make us feel good, as every story has a happy and "storybook" ending.[3] While all of this is well and good, imagine this Christmas without your child, a child that may have been senselessly killed. He cannot enjoy all the marvelous toys that department stores advertise. Imagine a husband, trying to stay upbeat and positive for his kids, as this will be the first Christmas without the beloved wife and mother, who "made Christmas" each and every year. Tom Hanks, in the movie, **Sleepless in Seattle**, tried to do this, and without much luck.

What can be done to help grieving families endure and survive the holidays? The following are some specific suggestions that, if acted upon, can give some sense of relief and purpose to the stressful holiday season. Although these suggestions are not a cure-all, they can bring some comfort and relief to a season that is usually stressful already.

REMEMBER THE RULES IN GRIEF AND LOSS

One needs to remember that there are "peaks" as well as "valleys" in loss. These valleys are the emotions and pains of the loss that come back at you, as if they happened just last week. Although it may have been several years since the time of the loss, these intense "peak" feelings make it seem as if the "wound" of the loss was fresh, as if it recently occurred. These intensified feelings often occur at the following times: six months after the loss, the one year anniversary of the death and loss, at eighteen months, and again at two years. They also surface during times of the major holidays, at the birthday of the deceased, and at one's anniversary in marriage.[4]

Therefore, if one feels bad during this time, it is natural and normal to do so. Rando suggests the idea that the anticipation of pain during the holidays is worse than the actual pain itself.[5] By preparing oneself for the pain and the distress that the holidays may bring, he may find that such preparation can serve as a buffer in helping him for what lies ahead.[6]

GIVE YOURSELF PERMISSION TO GRIEVE

When death comes and invades our life by taking away someone that was near and dear to us, it causes us to begin to live on a "primitive survival" level. Our thoughts turn inward, and rightly so. After all, as Doug Manning affirms, "Grief is the deepest wound you have ever had."[7] It is a major wound, and it will not go away simply because the holidays are here, and everyone should be jolly. It will intensify, because you cannot celebrate in the same way. The reason–your mate (or child or parent or sibling, etc.) is dead!

Many will enjoy the holiday season, but if you can just get through it, then you deserve a gold star. Some will not realize your loss, and others will have forgotten about it, but it is with you twenty-four hours a day, seven days a week. Therefore, be good to yourself, and treat yourself with extra-special care. If you had had major surgery, no one would expect you to run a marathon race in a month. If you broke a leg, no one would pity you for the use of crutches. The same should apply to grief. Regardless of what others think or do not think, give yourself permission to experience loneliness and sadness during the holidays.[8]

ALLOW YOURSELF TO BE "MERELY HUMAN"

At best, holiday times are a stressful season anyway. With the major addition of a significant loss to deal with, one can help himself greatly by choosing not to be "Superman or Superwoman" this year. Let others know what you can and cannot do this holiday season. You are not stating that every holiday will be like this from now on, but for this holiday season, this is the way it needs to be.

Allow others to help you this year. If you can tolerate the "tree" and the opening of the presents, then do so. At the same time, go ahead and declare, "I cannot handle Christmas Eve at my house, nor the big Christmas dinner. Someone else will need to do that." By proclaiming this, you let others know where you stand and what they can expect from you, and vice versa.[9]

Since you are "cutting back" this holiday season, be sure and work in some "down time" where you set aside some time for you and your thoughts. "These may be times for crying, for writing down your thoughts and feelings, or pretending that your loved one is in the room with you and saying out loud some of the things you wanted to say while he or she was alive."[10] Since your thoughts will be on your beloved, it is okay to admit this, and spend some time in thinking about and addressing your loss.

GIVE STRUCTURE TO YOUR HOLIDAYS, AS MUCH AS POSSIBLE

Why is it that we put so much stress on ourselves, rushing about trying to find the "perfect gift" for Aunt Harriet, when she has everything already? Seriously, there is a great deal of stress during the holiday season, and grief simply compounds it and makes it much greater. There are a few things that one might do to lessen the stress that they will feel.

First, plan your holiday time. If you do go out and shop for others, do it on a "good day" and try to do it all at once. Piece-mill holiday shopping can be very demanding as well as emotionally draining.

Second, declare that you are on a "stress-reduction diet" this holiday season. You plan not to over-spend, over-shop, over-worry, etc. Allow others to know that by simplifying Christmas plans as far as you are concerned, they can be of great help to you.[11]

Third, discuss holiday needs and tasks that are important to you with significant others, and then do them. Again, it is not being self-centered to let others know what is important to you this holiday season. If some ritual would be too stressful this year, let your wishes be known that we will forego this ritual for this year. To forego it one year does not mean that you cannot go back to it in the future. It simply says that a significant loss has taken place in your life, and you are wise enough to acknowledge that, and to make plans that will reduce stress in your troubled life this year.

CHANGE "SHOULDS" TO "WANTS"

At best, there will be some "eager beavers" who will try to plan your holiday gatherings for you. Some will think that the busier you stay, the better off you will be. Others might believe that to stay in and grieve is the proper thing to do.

Rather than allowing others to dictate your feelings for you, feel what you feel like doing and do it. If you want to attend a social gathering, and you end up enjoying it, then do so without guilt.[12] If you decide to leave town and do something entirely different, then go ahead and do so. Some may not think that you ought to, but they can "worry" about it the entire time you are gone. A dear sweet lady in one of my grief support classes lost her husband after fifty plus years of marriage. Always, at Christmas, they had stayed home and enjoyed the holiday with family that was nearby. Now for the first time, she was thinking of going out of state and enjoying Christmas with a son who had not been able to come home for Christmas for many years. "Some do not think that I should leave my present family, but what do you think?"

she asked. I told her, in the words of Doug Manning, to "feel what you feel."[13] If leaving town would bring her happiness and help in this difficult season, then she should do it. She was acknowledging that things could not be the same, no matter if she stayed at home or not. I believe she was making a wise decision.

As long as grieving people make decisions that are morally right and not harmful to them or others, they should do things that will help bring meaning and value to themselves during the holidays. If one wants to decorate a tree and place it near the cemetery plot of their beloved, then they should do so. If a special candle lit in the home or some special Christmas ornament will "lift up" the memory of the deceased, then by all means do it. This expresses to you and to others just how important that person was (and is) to you.[14]

If you have lost a mate, and you decide to attend a social gathering with a date, do not feel guilty over doing it. If you attend some gathering and actually catch yourself laughing or enjoying it, there is no need to feel bad. Re-investing ourselves emotionally with someone else does not mean that we have forgotten those that died. It is healthy grief that allows us in time, to re-invest our energies either in someone, or something.[15] Change your shoulds to wants and do them.

DO NOT BE AFRAID TO CHANGE TRADITIONS

As much as you would like to, there cannot be the bringing back of your beloved from the dead. You have suffered an irreversible loss, and that knowledge will stay with you during the holidays. To make this time as "painless" as possible, one might think of altering the "traditional" way they normally observe the holidays. If you have always had "Santa" on Christmas morning, then deliberately do it another time. Instead of having the traditional "Christmas" dinner, where the "empty chair" will be most noticeable, plan on going out to eat or having finger foods in another setting.

Some might suggest, that if "we do not do it just like we used to," we are desecrating the memory of the departed loved one. This is not true at all-all you are trying to do is acknowledge the fact that they have died, and that you are trying to make it through the holidays, the best way you know how. Changing traditions does not mean that you are "wallowing in grief," or that you are a nervous wreck. Neither is there some unwritten rule that says you cannot go back to that tradition next year, or later in the future. Perhaps the death of your loved one should cause you to reevaluate your traditions, with the idea of deciding which ones you might want to carry on, and what new tradition you might want to begin in memory of the deceased.[16] One mother regularly cooked gingerbread houses every Christmas. When her children were killed, she found that she could not cook them the first Christmas after their deaths. The next year, and for years later, she did bake them and gave them as gifts to friends who had meant a great deal to her.[17]

With traditions, one has to think about children or little grand-children. They may not understand why you are not having Christmas "just like before," so forethought and planning will have to go into making Christmas as special as possible for them. In some cases, they may be the ones who are hurting the most. A good rule of thumb is to make holiday plans in accordance to the survivors who are hurting the most.[18]

STRIVE FOR A BALANCED LIFESTYLE

Under normal circumstances, holidays can be stressful at best. Add bereavement to the holidays, and "emotional overload" can easily become a reality. Be good to yourself during this special time of the year. Do your best to get plenty of rest. Reading, watching TV, taking long baths, or just going for a long walk may be exactly what you need for comfort.[19] Try not to overeat, or overdo anything. Alcohol is a depressant, so one should not partake of that which will make them feel worse, not better.[20]

COMFORT CAN BE FOUND IN DOING THINGS FOR OTHERS

As part of a new tradition, one might think of some special gift that could be given in memory and in honor of the deceased. Perhaps, there was a special work that was near and dear to them. If so, a gift given in their memory would help the recipients. as well as allow the memory of the deceased to continue. We know that memories will forever remain-no one can take that from us. In the words of Henry Ward Beecher, "what heart has once owned and had, it shall never lose."[21] Yet a gift given in their memory can keep on giving for years to come, and help someone in the process.

In one of the classes I taught, a lady lost her husband suddenly as he died of a heart attack. He was a self-taught computer programmer, and was always involved in the work of the church in that capacity. His desire was to work at the church, updating and maximizing the use of computers for the good of the congregation. His unexpected death did not allow him to fulfill his dreams. In his memory, the family bought a new computer system for the congregation, something that the husband had always wanted to do. This allowed his good name to live on, as well as profit the church. Another lady in my class gave money for the building of shelves for the new church library. Her husband had loved books, and now at his death, his memory could live on through her gracious generosity.

COUNTER THE CONSPIRACY OF SILENCE

One needs to remember that at holiday season, friends and consolers may do and say all the wrong things. Some may talk about the deceased, asking questions and making statements, when you prefer that they would not.[22] Some, thinking that they know just what to do and say, may really get on your nerves the most. Others may not say anything to you at all, even when you bring up the subject, and you would like for them to reminisce of good memories that you have of the deceased.[23]

For that reason, let it be known whether you want to talk about the deceased or not. If you do, and most likely you will, then let it be known that it is okay to tell of special memories that are pleasant or sweet. This will cause the avoidance of "uncomfortable" pauses in conversation at social gatherings, etc.[24]

KEEP YOUR FAITH

Take time during the holidays to reflect on your faith. Accept the blessings that are yours because of your faith. Your loss has caused you to re-examine your faith, asking hard questions about death, loss, love, God, yourself, and others. Although some questions may never be answered, one should pause to thank God for the blessings that are theirs, realizing that "He is our refuge and strength, a very present help in trouble."(Ps. 46:1) Although your loss has caused you to have a different perception, even of God, it is helpful to realize that He still loves us, that He cares for us, that He is the "God of all comfort" (2 Cor. 1:3), and that He hurts with us, because of our loss.[25]

CONCLUSION

I would love to paint a rosy picture for folks who come to my grief class, looking for some relief, when the holidays come their way. Sadly, there is only so much that can be done to relieve the heartache and pain. It is my opinion that these ten suggestions will aid in alleviating some of the great distress that can occur during the holiday season, while at the same time giving proper tribute to a life that was lived, and is still alive, within our hearts.

Try as we may, we cannot change what has happened in the past. "You can take charge of the present, however. And you can shape the future. Total recovery may never come. But what you make of the ashes of your trauma is up to you."[26]

WORKS CITED

1   Janice Harris Lord, **No Time for Goodbyes**, (Ventura, California: Pathfinder Publishing, 1987), p. 98.

2   Therese A. Rando, **How to go on Living When Someone you Love Dies**, (New York: Bantam Books,1988), p. 289.

3   Lord, 98.

4   Doug Manning, Cassette Tape on "Grief and the Holidays", 1992.

5   Rando, 289.

6   Doug Manning, Cassette Tape.

7   Doug Manning, **Don't Take my Grief Away from Me**, (Hereford, Texas: Insight Books, 1979,), p. 68.

8   Ibid, 65.

9   Sally Featherstone, Handout on "Holiday Survivorship Skills", p. 1.

10   Lord, 100.

11   Manning, Tape.

12   Featherstone, Handout.

13   Manning, Tape.

14   Rando, 290.

15   Randy Becton, Tract entitled "Preparing People for the Holidays", p. 4.

16   Rando, 290.

17   Lord, 101.

18   Ibid, 99.

19   Featherstone,1.

20   Linda Sewell, Handout on "Grief and the Holidays", Hospice of Northwest Alabama, p. 2.

21   Ibid.

22   Lord, 100.

23   Becton, 5.

24   Lord, 100,101.

25   Sewell, 3.

26   Lord, 102.

Chapter 13

Will I Make It Through The Night?

What Grievers Ought To Know About "Turning The Corner"

by Don Williams

O n a Sunday afternoon, a preacher was getting settled down to watch the Cowboys-Redskins football game on television when his phone rang. The caller told him that a close friend had accidentally run over his own three year old son. Upon rushing to the hospital, he found the father and took him outside to talk to him. As the father collapsed on the hospital lawn, he cried out, "Jack, will I ever laugh again?"[1]

The question asked by the distressed father is one that all grievers ask. Grievers wonder if they will ever experience a happy day again. Feelings of guilt may surface at the very thought that the survivors might enjoy a day or days of happiness and joy. Throughout one's journey in grief, feelings of guilt or betrayal will "pop up" as one works through the grief and continues to exist. As Grollman puts it, "Death brings you a choice. It can lead you to the edge of the abyss. Or you can build a bridge that will span the chasm."[2] In making that choice to live as meaningful a life as possible, one makes the best of a bad situation.

> You may not have completely regained your balance. Yet life continues, though scars remain. You are breathing, moving, functioning. You are now able to remember the one you

loved, and the circumstances surrounding the death, without falling apart.[3]

There is a point in the grief journey when grievers "turn the corner." That is, they work through the intense emotions of grief and decide to live. Although bad days still occur (and will occur), one goes on with life, accepting the consequences that death has dealt them. Clark, in her book, **Are You Weeping with Me, God?**, describes this "turning of the corner" when she writes,

> Now, when friends drop by, I smile, I talk of days to come, and I laugh. Perhaps not as joyous a laugh as I once had, but still a laugh. Occasionally, I go with them to shop and to meet other friends. They probably know that I still grieve, but rarely does it come into our conversation. And I accept that, for I have been places they have not been and felt pain they could not know...Hour by hour, day by day, grace sufficient. Now I understand. I am not the same, God, but I think I am on the way back.[4]

How does one turn the corner? How do grievers get to the point of seeing the light at "the end of the tunnel?" What roads must one take in order to desire to live again? In this final chapter, a discussion of tasks that must be accomplished to turn the corner will be discussed. Also, steps that determine that one is moving toward the future will be given.

FOUR MAJOR TASKS OF GRIEF

In order to work through grief, the first task is to come to face with the fact that the loved one has died and will not return. Although denial is a common phase that one goes through, one must reach the point where the reality of the loss is accepted.[5] Grollman writes, "Your loved one is dead. It may not be fair, but it is a fact that has to be accepted. You cannot bring that person back again to life."[6]

The second task is to learn to experience the pain of grief. Grief is often referred to as work, and rightly so. It is demanding of one's time and energies, and affects a person socially, physically, mentally, and spiritually. Someone has rightly said that "grief is to loss what healing is to surgery." When one breaks an arm or leg, one can only recover full use of that limb through rigorous therapy. That therapy will be painful at times, but it is necessary for the growth and desired well-being of the patient. The same is true of grief. It must be worked with and worked through.

Another statement worth mentioning is this: "Attempting to suppress grief is like trying to cover cancer with a bandaid." Denying the feelings of grief, whether it be guilt, denial, anger, loneliness, or other emotions, only delays the griever from properly working through his grief.[7] Often the statement is made that time will take care of all wounds caused by grief. Of this Grollman writes,

> Time heals, many people say. It may. It may help to dull your pain. But the medicine of time, taken by itself, is not sure. Time is neutral. What helps is what you do with time...Are you using the time to give vent to your fears and anxieties? Are you using the time to create a capacity for enjoyment without feeling guilty?..You must help time to do its healing.[8]

Only when one fully experiences the pain caused by grief can one begin the road to recovery and reconciliation.

The third task in working through grief is to adjust to the environment in which the deceased is no longer present. For different survivors, it means different things. This writer attended a funeral today of a older man who died suddenly. The deceased was survived by a wife, children, and siblings. It will be difficult for the wife to adjust to the situation where her beloved is no longer present. Whereas children and siblings have families to "go back home to," each will have to adjust to a lifestyle without the father or brother present. Although this task will often take a great deal of time and energy, it is necessary in the grief journey that leads to recovery.[9]

The final task of grieving is to emotionally relocate the deceased within their life and move on with a new life. This involves withdrawing some of the emotion that was invested in their love, and re-investing it elsewhere. For some, it may be with another human being. For others, it may be new hobbies or a new occupation. This usually requires a great deal of time, and will come only after the other tasks have been worked through successfully.[10]

In no sense does this task suggests that the deceased is forgotten. It is not possible to forget someone who made such an impression on one's life.

> Those things that are important to you in your life are remembered and kept in the very special places of your heart and mind. This is no less true in regard to the loss of a beloved person. Keep this loss, treasure what you have learned from it, take the memories that you have from the person and the relationship and, in a healthy fashion, remember what should be remembered, hold on to what should be retained, and let go of that which must be relinquished. And then, as you continue on to invest emotionally in other people, goals, and pursuits, appropriately take your loved one with you, along with your new sense of self and new way

of relating to the world, to enrich your present and future life without forgetting your important past.[11]

How is this task accomplished? As one works through the grief and begins to reconcile himself to the reality of the present situation, one may begin to reinvest emotions in other areas. There may have to be the saying of good-bye before there is a saying of hello. As Manning suggests in his book, **Don't take my Grief away from Me**, "Growth is saying good-bye and saying hello."[12]

One way this can be accomplished is in the writing of a letter to the deceased. Grief support facilitators have suggested this to grieving families, especially when the loss was sudden, and there was insufficient time to say good-bye. Losses where the relationship was less than ideal might also warrant a letter to the deceased, exposing failures on the part of both parties. The reason for such a letter would be to examine one's relationship with the deceased, and to complete one's emotional relationship with that loved one.[10] Another way of saying good-bye might be in the cleaning out of the loved one's possessions and/or clothes. Cleaning out drawers, sorting through mementos, going through the loved one's desk; these are ways that one can work so as to begin to say good-bye to a former life and hello to a new life.

When is mourning finished? Asking such a question is like asking how high is up? In a sense, mourning is never complete. There will be various feelings of grief that one will experience at different times in their life. One benchmark of a completed grief reaction is when the person is able to think of the deceased without pain. There may always be a sense of sadness when thinking of the deceased loved one, but the wrenching sadness is no longer present.[14]

In a survey conducted of six hundred families who

had suffered a loss of a loved one, factors were determined as to how these families moved on from their significant loss. These common actions surfaced. First, they found someone with whom they could share their loss and talk. Secondly, they as grievers made a cognitive decision to work through and get beyond their grief. Third, they determined to clean up any relationships that were presently lacking. Fourth, they determined to live in the present. Finally, they learned that in order to have they had to give.

SIGNS OF MOVING TOWARD THE FUTURE

"You've made it. You are out of the house. You continue to exist. Not like before. Not the way you would choose-if you had a choice. But you are beginning again."[15] Such thoughts suggest that one is moving toward a new life and a new beginning.

A person is moving toward the future when small changes begin to be made. The first dinner out with others, the motivation to clean one's house again, the desire to get back into shopping-all of these suggest that a person is beginning to live again.

Another sign that one is moving toward the future is when there is a decrease in the need to protect family members. Often in grief, there is the overwhelming urge to "shelter" children or adults in the family from the pain of grief. While this may be possible for a short while, there is a time when all must begin to deal with the trauma of the loss. One is moving toward the future when there is no longer a need to protect others.

One is moving toward the future when they have the ability to think of others. No longer is the focus on themselves, but on the needs of others and how they can be helped.[16] Commenting on this point, Grollman writes,

One touch of sorrow makes the whole world kin. At first you have to force yourself to leave the security of your house in order to share somebody else's problems. Is it worth the effort? You have enough of your own grief. Why burden yourself with the grief of others? ...Because you, yourself, have experienced grief, you are better able to understand the heartache of others. As you lift a hand to help another, you are lifting yourself.[17]

Another sign of moving toward the future includes an increased capability to deal with emotions without becoming incapacitated. At first, the emotions of grief can make one feel incompetent, almost as in a vacuum. Grievers have described their lives as almost an "out of the body" experience, as if they are daydreaming. As one works through the grief, they begin to be able to handle the flurry of emotions without feeling "swallowed up."

Another sign that one is moving toward the future is genuine interest in being with old friends, as well as a desire to make new friends. One is no longer willing to "hibernate in grief," but is willing to take the "risk" of getting out in public and being involved in old activities, as well as establishing a desire for involvement in new activities.

A final sign that one is moving toward the future is when the ability and desire to "have fun" without feeling guilty returns. One has worked through the "maze" of grief and now sees the "light" at the end of the tunnel. There is a reason to live, and one can now look forward to life without the feeling of guilt or betrayal. Living life to the fullest is not dishonoring the memory of the deceased, but is rather a testimony to a relationship that was begun and nurtured when they were alive. Continuing that good life is a way of memorializing that relationship and keeping that loved one alive, at least in memory.[18]

CONCLUSION

How can grievers make the journey through grief, and turn the corner at the end of the journey? One can only do so by having a great deal of courage, commitment, and love, not only for the deceased, but also for themselves. As Grollman writes,

> Courage is not the absence of fear and pain, but the affirmation of life despite fear and pain. No matter how great the pain, there is hope and help for the future. As your sense of humor returns and you find yourself laughing, you're feeling better. As you begin to make major decisions about your life, you're getting better still. When you are able to take out the mementos of your beloved and smile through your tears at memories of happiness together, you're much improved. And when you learn that no one can bring back your loved one, that it's your job to pick up and go on living, then you'll know you are truly growing and recovering yourself.[19]

Several years ago, Dr. Henri Nouwen coined the phrase "wounded healer." Nouwen suggests that grievers are at their best when they are willing to expose their own pain while dealing with the pain of others. He writes,

> I am a wounded healer-someone who has had to look carefully after my own wounds while at the same time caring enough to try to do something in the name of Christ about the wounds of others.[20]

Many grievers have suggested that in helping others, they too were helped. Truly, the journey of grief equips those who have traveled that way with experience and feelings which others who have not traveled that way know very little. The purpose of this book has been to supply information that will help grievers and caregivers on their journey. It is a journey that will one day be traveled by all. Because some have traveled through grief and come out on the other side, it is possible for others to make that same journey and survive as well. Jack Reese suggests that in one's journey,

> ...don't lose sight of the suffering God, the God who relinquished his own son...in our tragedy, his was the first heart broken. It is Christ who weeps with us just as he wept with Lazarus. Part of the Good News is that God suffers with us, feels our pain.[21]

Will grievers ever laugh again? Reese concludes by saying, "It has been three years since my friend and I cried on the lawn. I saw him at church Sunday. I was greeting visitors at the foyer door. He whispered an 'inside' joke. We laughed raucously."[22]

WORKS CITED

1 Jack R. Reese, "Will I ever Laugh Again?", **Twentieth Century Christian**, (Volume 49, August 1987), p. 4.

2 Earl A. Grollman, **Living When a Loved one has Died**, (Boston: Beacon Press, 1977), p. 106.

3 Ibid, 109.

4 Martha Bittle Clark, **Are You Weeping with Me, God?**, (Nashville: Broadman Press, 1987), p. 93.

5 J. William Worden, **Grief Counselling and Grief Therapy**, (New York: Springer Publishing, 1991), pp. 10,11.

6 Earl A. Grollman, Editor, **What Helped Me when My Loved one Died**, (Boston: Beacon Press, 1981), p.149.

7 Worden, 13.

8 Grollman, Living, 76,77.

9 Worden, 14,15.

10 Ibid, 16.

11 Therese A. Rando, **How to go on Living When Someone You Love Dies**, (New York: Bantam Books, 1988), p. 287.

12 Doug Manning, **Don't Take My Grief Away from Me**, (Hereford, Texas: Insight Books, 1979), p. 120.

13 Worden, 148,149.

14 Worden, 18.

15 Earl A. Grollman, Editor, **What Helped Me when My Loved one Died**, (Boston: Beacon Press, 1981), p.83.

16 Handout used with Permission entitled "Signs of Moving Toward the Future," East Tennessee Children's Hospital Social Services Department.

17 Grollman, Living, 102-104.

18 Handout, "Signs of Moving..."

19 Grollman, What Helped, 149, 150.

20 Dr. Henri Nouwen, **The Wounded Healer**, (New York: Doubleday Publishing, 1974), p. 40.

21 Reese, 6.

22 Ibid.

AVAILABLE WORKSHOPS

Grief Workshops
Dementia & Alzheimer's Seminar
Cancer Seminar

These workshops are designed to help the **patient** and/or **caregiver**,
while educating others so they can better help those who are suffering.
The topics can be presented **alone** or **in any combination**
that best meets the needs of your congregation.
The workshops are most effective in a **2-day** format
(but can be condensed into **1 day**, if necessary).

- ❖ **Ron & Don** have taught **Grief Support Classes** for over **25 years**.
- ❖ They have conducted **2-day Grief Workshops** together (or alone) in **70 congregations** in **11 states**.
- ❖ **Ron** has done extensive **Cancer** Research & has taught Support Classes for Cancer since 2012.
- ❖ **Don** has done extensive Research in the field of **Dementia & Alzheimer's** & has conducted Seminars on this subject since 2008.
- ❖ **Ron & Don** are now conducting **2-day Seminars** on Cancer & Dementia for congregations who have members dealing with these dreaded diseases.

For More Information ...
Or To Set Up A Seminar For Your Congregation ...

Contact Ron: ron@lincolnchurch.org   **Don**: donwill55@yahoo.com
1307 Meridian Street   62 Ridgecrest Lane
Huntsville, AL 35801   Killen, AL 35645

You may also visit our website at www.rondonbooks.com for more information

✻ ✻ ✻ ✻ ✻ ✻ ✻ ✻ ✻ ✻ ✻ ✻ ✻ ✻ ✻ ✻ ✻ ✻ ✻

Walking With Those Who Weep is also available
in an **E-read Format** & can be purchased from **Amazon.com**.